I0438503

# POWER PARENTS

*Children and Sex*

KGOSI DORAN MD
AND KOPO DORAN RN APRN

authorHOUSE®

*AuthorHouse*™
*1663 Liberty Drive*
*Bloomington, IN 47403*
*www.authorhouse.com*
*Phone: 1-800-839-8640*

© *2012 by Kgosi Doran MD and Kopo Doran RN APRN. All rights reserved.*

*No part of this book may be reproduced, stored in a retrieval system, or transmitted by any means without the written permission of the author.*

*Published by AuthorHouse    04/14/2012*

*ISBN: 978-1-4685-7387-9 (sc)*
*ISBN: 978-1-4685-7386-2 (e)*

*Any people depicted in stock imagery provided by Thinkstock are models, and such images are being used for illustrative purposes only.*
*Certain stock imagery © Thinkstock.*

*This book is printed on acid-free paper.*

*Because of the dynamic nature of the Internet, any web addresses or links contained in this book may have changed since publication and may no longer be valid. The views expressed in this work are solely those of the authors and do not necessarily reflect the views of the publisher, and the publisher hereby disclaims any responsibility for them.*

# DEDICATION

This book is written for the youth of Botswana, who will lead us tomorrow. We must maximize their potential and assure their future.

## WHO SHOULD READ THIS BOOK?

Parents, Guardians, Students, Youth Leaders, Aunts, Uncles, Grandparents, Teachers, Health Professionals, Social Workers, Counselors, Peer Educators and all who care for youth.

# ABOUT THE AUTHORS

KGOSI AND KOPO Doran are American Peace Corps Volunteers who served in Botswana from 2009-2011 and were always known by their Setswana names. In America, Christopher M. Doran MD and Maureen O. Doran RN APRN are medical and mental health professionals. Dr. Doran is a board-certified Psychiatrist, a Distinguished Fellow of the American Psychiatric Association and the author of three other books. Maureen Doran is a board-certified Advanced Practice Psychiatric Nurse and the recipient of numerous awards including the Outstanding Faculty Teaching Award at the University of Colorado School of Medicine, the Department of Veterans Affairs Excellence in Nursing Award and the Outstanding Nurse Clinician in the State of Colorado. In addition to 30 years of experience treating adults, families, and adolescents, each of the Doran's is a Clinical Professor at the University of Colorado Health Sciences Center.

In addition to writing this book, the Doran's have presented numerous lectures and workshops on a variety of topics to students, teachers, guidance counselors, and community groups in Botswana. They also served as visiting faculty at the University of Botswana Medical School in 2010 and 2011.

# ACKNOWLEDGEMENTS

THE AUTHORS WISH to acknowledge with special thanks Ms. Peggy McClure, the former Peace Corps Country Director in Botswana for her encouragement with the original idea and paving the way within the Peace Corps experience to allow time for this book to be written. Also we want to acknowledge the efforts of our counterparts in Botswana—Semakaleng Ooke, the Ramotswa District AIDS Coordinator and the District AIDS Coordinator's Office staff including Nthami Chilisa and Lesedi Mpuchane, as well as Ngwakwana Malema, Head of the Guidance Department at Kagiso Senior Secondary School in Ramotswa. They have supported this project and generously carved out time within our regular assignments allowing us to write.

It has been a labor of love to write this book and we hope that it will serve as a beacon of understanding, learning and instruction for the peoples of Botswana and Africa for many years to come.

CMD, MOD

# Authors' Note

The characters Kefentse, Tsiamo, their families and friends are purely fictional and created by the authors. Any connection to real persons, living or dead is purely coincidental. The villages in Botswana mentioned in the book and the University of Botswana are real places which serve as settings for this fictional story. The authors do not intend to represent that any of the events in this story actually occurred in these places.

# INTRODUCTION

TIMES HAVE CHANGED—RAPIDLY and drastically. The 21$^{st}$ century is not the Botswana of even 15 years ago. Becoming parents and raising children in the age of HIV, AIDS and other Sexually Transmitted Illnesses (STI's) is tremendously challenging. More than ever it is crucially important for parents and parents-to-be to be fully aware of the needs of children and teens when considering issues of sexual health, sexual illnesses and sexual behavior.

WE CANNOT WAIT. Our children and teens need us NOW.

Their health, happiness and possibly their survival require us to be actively informed and communicating. Parents and children must participate in important discussions about sexuality. Today's parents cannot rely on the "old ways" of parental behavior. The Botswana cultural practice of parents not talking with their children, talking in metaphors, and avoiding issues of sexuality is no longer safe—the stakes are too high. It is too dangerous for our children to face the challenges of making smart sexual decisions without accurate information, sound guidance and strong moral principles. We must be active in their lives and open to the sensitive issues of sex and sexuality. Each of us must become a "Power Parent" to our children.

This book serves as a challenge to the parents and parents-to-be of Botswana and a wakeup call to many others—Change, Adapt and Succeed! We must do so to help our nation thrive and take its rightful place in the modern world. *Power Parents* can save our children's lives.

Students can help their parents now by reading and discussing this book with them. Many students will become parents themselves. They can prepare themselves to be parents who give their children the best opportunity for health and success by understanding the concepts and dialogues suggested in this book.

A Power Parent today utilizes the best of what is already known about raising children, while learning new ideas, approaches and techniques. Besides being a guide book, this is the story of Kefentse and Tsiamo. Their story provides a roadmap for parents in helping children grow into adults who are healthy, happy and confident in their roles as men and women.

Kefentse and Tsiamo have the same challenges that all parents and couples face. It took courage on their part to become Power Parents, and the road was difficult. But that's getting ahead of ourselves . . .

# CHAPTER 1

## Gaborone, Block 7, 9:30 PM

KEFENTSE SAT ON her patio in the early autumn twilight; there was a growing chill in the air. The children were peacefully sleeping in their bedrooms, but her mind raced and was filled with emotion. She had just angrily banished her husband to a place six hundred kilometers away. At least for now, she did not want him coming back to this, their Gaborone home—it was too painful. She knew she could not dwell on this event for too long though. Problems with her 16 year old daughter, Kagiso, also pressed her with anxiety. Kagiso, a sweet child who had turned insolent and angry as a teen, was in trouble. She was dodging school and Kefentse had begun to wonder if the girl was secretly involved with a man. As her parent, she knew that she was going to have to confront these issues head-on. As always, she had the will, but now she also needed the words to speak to her daughter. It hurt to think of serious problems with two of the most important people in her life. They were both like open wounds—too fresh to take on tonight after such a long and draining day. She knew where she would find the roadmap and words to deal with her family, but she needed to start when she was fresh in the morning. She wanted to think about something else.

Without really intending to, she found herself drifting into memories of her earlier life and all that led up to where she was now . . .

*She had been the fourth child and initially the only girl in her family, born in the village of Rakops just north of the Central Kalahari Game Reserve. The year was 1980, just 14 years after Botswana's independence. She remembered her birth year because as she grew, her parents kept talking* about how proud they were that Botswana had become an independent nation in a peaceful manner. Her father often would boast about Botswana's developing economic prosperity because diamonds had been discovered. "Just think Kefentse, when you were born in 1980, we had been an independent country for only 14 years. Before we had been a poor nation and look at us now!"

Much of the progress was not evident in the small village of Rakops. When they visited their relatives in Francistown and Maun however, Kefentse could see the paved roads, the big buildings and the cars. She remembered envying her cousins who lived in these places. They had nicer clothes than she, and their parents had government jobs. Her uncle wore a shirt and tie to work and could get a driver to take him to meetings. She felt embarrassed about her old clothes and worn sandals. But at least her family was good to their children and only lightly beat them occasionally.

For the first 9 years, Kefentse's upbringing had been relatively unremarkable. As a girl, she had cooking and household responsibilities which she learned and performed well. When her younger sister Refilwe was born, Kefentse was also happily tasked with some motherly duties for her baby sister. She would have enjoyed learning about cattle, hunting and riding donkeys, but that instruction was given by her father to her older brothers. Time passed and as she grew, it became clear to everyone in the family and in her village that she was an exceptionally beautiful child who was appealing in every way.

Although education was not a high priority for her family, she managed to complete Standard 3, with average grades. She was accepted into Standard 4 at the local school. While not the most advanced student in class, she was far from the lowest. She liked to look at books and was beginning to read well. She had a curious mind, a practical cleverness and a persistence to get a task done when she set her mind to it. Kefentse loved the idea that one day she could become a successful woman. She dreamed that when she was older she would live and work in a big city like Francistown.

Then it happened—the Saturday she would never forget. Her father came into the house crying, gathered the children together and told them, "Your mother has been killed by a truck as she was walking along the road to the village." Kefentse could not believe it. She loved her Mother so much.

The funeral and the next several months were a blur of sadness, crying and grief. Her Father decided that Kefentse must leave school and stay home to care for Refilwe. At only 10 years of age Kefentse became a mother figure and primary caretaker. She was required to become very efficient and expert in the tasks of running a household. At first she didn't know where to start and felt overwhelmed, but she knew she had to grow up fast. There was really no choice. Kefentse asked for help from her aunts and received practical advice on caring for Refilwe, shopping, food preparation, washing clothes, cleaning the yard and keeping the home for her family. She had to adapt and change from being a child into being a caregiver overnight. It was very hard, but with her industrious nature and willingness to work, she took on the role with increasing success. She had little time for herself, but when she did, she looked at whatever magazines she could find, trying to make herself a better reader. She often lay awake at night letting her thoughts go to bigger, better places than Rakops while trying to avoid the ache for her Mother that she still felt in her heart.

Time moved ahead slowly. Her Father, who was a decent and hard-working man, attracted the attention of several unattached women in the village. They knew he still had young children to raise and more than one of them hinted that she would help with childrearing if he would support her and be her partner. Any such decision though, had to be approved by her Father's parents and grandparents. Eventually the elders selected a woman named Dintle who came into the home. Dintle began doing many of the wifely chores including the care of Refilwe.

With a grown woman in the house, Kefentse was able to return to school, which pleased her very much. She grew into a young adolescent and was delighted to have more time to play and just be a child, not the mother of the house. Dintle was pleasant and quiet, but she was not Kefentse's mother—no one could replace her Mother. The closest adult woman she knew and loved was Aunt Naledi, her Mother's sister. Naledi was a librarian in Gaborone and had supported Kefentse in all ways including encouragement for Kefentse's love *of learning. Although it was not frequent, whenever they got together, her Aunt would give Kefentse things to read. Without anyone ever telling her, Kefentse knew that learning was an important part of growing up and would be the path to a job in the big city. Since she was now less tired from being responsible to do all the chores, Kefentse would often stay up reading until dark, even when it hurt her eyes. Stories were so interesting. They could easily transport her away from Rakops into magical worlds and away from the pain that she still felt when she thought of her Mother.*

*Kefentse's parents had participated in initiation schools and ceremonies but this tradition had decreased in Botswana. Although she was approaching the age for Bojale, the adolescent girl initiation, this rite was discontinued so she never went. She had been told that these events helped children learn things about becoming an adult. Since she never attended and the initiations were very secret, she never knew what was talked about or what knowledge might have been passed on there.*

*One day, she noticed blood coming between her legs. She was scared and thought she might be really sick. She didn't know what to do and was very nervous for several days until it decreased and stopped. All seemed well for a month and she almost forgot about it, when it suddenly happened again. As before, it stopped in 4-5 days.*

*This time however, Dintle noticed Kefentse's bloody clothing and said that the time had come to have a visit from nkukuagwe, Kefentse's maternal grandmother, who lived in the village of Molepolole. Kefentse had seen nkukuagwe on family trips and at her Mother's funeral, but did not know her well. When visiting nkukuagwe, Kefentse would play with the other children while the adult women cooked and chatted among themselves. Now Kefentse was afraid. Why would nkukuagwe be called to see her and what would she say to her?*

*Later that week as Saturday approached, Kefentse became even more nervous as her father traveled to Molepolole to bring nkukuagwe to their home. As she entered the house, Kefentse noticed that nkukuagwe had aged since the death of her daughter, Kefentse's Mother. Her skin, once smooth and beautiful, now looked wrinkled and tired. She walked with a stoop in her back, slowly and with some difficulty. Her traditional blanket covered shoulders that once had been broad and strong, but now looked narrow and sagged. The grandmother greeted Dintle, Kefentse and the other children and was given the seat of honor in the sitting room. After some chatting, all of the family left as Dintle brought tea for Kefentse and nkukuagwe, then left the room. After they had sipped the tea, nkukuagwe turned to Kefentse.*

*"I have come at a very special time in your life, Kefentse" said nkukuagwe. "Dintle has told me what has happened—your bleeding has started. Your strong body is now the body of a woman. As in the history of all your female ancestors and in the future lives of all your sisters, you have now grown from a girl to a woman. From this time forward, you will be able to accept the seed of a man and become a mother. You are as fertile as the lands in the early spring."*

*Kefentse felt hypnotized by the musical voice and words of nkukuagwe. While her body had aged, Kefentse noted the brightness and clarity of nkukuagwe's eyes. They studied Kefentse, never leaving her face as she spoke words that had been passed down among Batswana women for generations.*

*Nkukuagwe reached for the bag she had carried from Molepolole. She untied the draw-string top and carefully brought out a towel that was covering something small. Nkukuagwe removed the faded covering and Kefentse's eyes widened. There emerged the most beautiful blue bowl she had ever seen. The small creation sparkled in the sun and the design was of flowers that had been cut into the clay. It was stunning.*

*"This bowl was given to your mother when she became a woman. I saved it for you after she was late. It has been in our family since the British first arrived in our country. A wealthy English woman gave it to my grandmother's mother as a gift before returning to her home in Britain. They had shared a special relationship because my great grandmother raised the children of this woman. The bowl represents thankfulness and love. Since that time, it has represented all that is pure and good about becoming a woman. Just as you treasure this bowl, so you must value your body. You must treasure your body and not let it be damaged or stained."*

Nkukuagwe handed the beautiful gift to Kefentse who was trembling at the words and meaning of this treasure. She would never forget this moment. She knew that she was special. She now knew that being a woman was special too. Nkukuagwe went on to say that the bleeding she was having was "normal" and that she did not need to worry. As was the tradition, children could, if they wanted, ask a mosadi mogolo questions about such things, but there was little encouragement for children to speak up. They often did not even know what questions to ask. Kefentse did not understand how it could be "normal" to be bleeding every month, but she also knew that questions from children were not welcomed by adults. Like other children in the 1990's, Kefentse kept her thoughts to herself.

While showing her how to manage the bleeding with cloths, nkukuagwe also said, "Since you are fertile, you must now be very careful with boys." Kefentse had no idea what this meant, but it bothered her because she had grown up loving her three older brothers. She liked playing with them and doing things they did. Now that Dintle was in the house, if her chores were done, she also enjoyed spending time with both the village boys and girls. She often kicked the football with the boys and was even allowed to join in their games when they didn't have enough boy players. But now, Kefentse was confused. Should she be afraid of boys? Again, all she really knew was that children were meant to listen to their elders and obey.

For the next two years Kefentse was content to be in school, do her chores and spend most of her time with her sister and the other girls in the village. There was no library in her town, but whenever she visited her cousins in Francistown, she would go to the library there and spend hours looking through the books, trying to learn about new and exciting things.

One day when she was 15 and walking to the village shops, she noticed a good looking boy from the other side. She had not seen him before, but saw that he seemed to be looking closely at her as she passed by. She thought he was handsome and asked her girlfriends about him. The friends did not know much about the boy except that he was the youngest of four brothers, and came from a good family. His name was Gape. Kefentse would have liked to meet him, but knew that girls were not supposed to have "boyfriends" at her age.

One day, when she was again walking to the shops, Gape came up to her and started to walk alongside. They chatted easily, and he asked many questions about her and her family. When they arrived at the general dealer, he left, but asked her when she would be coming back. She said that it would be next Saturday. This began a routine, where they would meet and talk as they walked to and from her house. On the way back, Gape always stopped and left her before they got to her gate, so her family would not notice a boy walking with her. One evening, as they were returning home near dusk, he reached out and held her hand. Her heart leapt in her chest and she was thrilled that he seemed interested in her. She talked with her girlfriends about this joyous feeling. Was this falling in love? Could this be the man of her dreams? She asked them about how she should "be careful" around boys, but received very different answers from each of the girls. She was as confused as ever.

By the time she was 16, Kefentse was making every effort to spend time with Gape. She still did not mention him to her father or Dintle. Her girlfriends all knew that Gape was Kefentse's boyfriend but this was something they kept secret as friends. Since Gape was three years older and very good looking, Kefentse's friends were happy and some were even a bit jealous of their relationship. The friends spoke often about how lucky she was to have found someone, but the conversations were idle girl chatter. None of the girls really knew how to be with a man, how to please a man or how a man should act with a woman. Beyond the gossiping with her girlfriends, Kefentse could not tell anyone in her family about this relationship. She could not even tell her little sister how wonderful she felt when she was with Gape.

One Saturday, Kefentse and Gape walked to the outskirts of the village and sat together under a Mokopi tree. After some small talk, Gape suddenly reached over and kissed her. Kefentse was flustered and did not quite know what to do, but knew that she liked being kissed by him and wanted to kiss him back, which she did. She suddenly felt a curious mix of pleasure and guilt.

*She remembered nkukuagwe's words and the beautiful, untarnished bowl. She got up abruptly and started walking back toward town, leaving Gape surprised and disappointed . . .*

Suddenly Kefentse awoke from her daydreaming. She realized that it was almost midnight. It had been a long hard day since she had told Tsiamo to leave. She needed sleep.

# CHAPTER 2

## The University of Botswana campus; Year 1 Day 4

TSIAMO TRIED TO fit his lanky frame into the one-piece desk and chair in the large University classroom, but he was too tall to find a comfortable position. Eventually, he more slouched than sat, extending his legs to the side as he looked around the room. It would be 20 minutes before class was to begin and the chairs began to fill. As he glanced around, he wondered how many of the young men were going to try out for the football team. He worried that the skills he had refined in secondary school would not be sufficient for the University team. He spotted a muscular, athletically built boy several rows ahead and began thinking to himself, "That guy looks really strong. There is going to be a lot of competition here." When he didn't see any other likely athletes, he returned to his assignment, reading it again, line by line for the third time.

It was the second class of his first year English course at the University of Botswana. The class assignment for the students had been to write a narrative about their lives prior to coming to University. The professor had said that the assignment had two purposes. He wanted to both assess the student's writing skills and he wanted them to read their papers to the class as a way to get to know one another. As he traditionally had done with all his school work, Tsiamo had worked hard on the paper and had revised it several times. He wanted to make a good start academically. Tsiamo was the third one chosen to read his paper to the class.

## TSIAMO'S LIFE

From a young age, I have been one of the most successful people at most everything I have done. I am confident and I like to be a leader. I was born in Serowe in 1977 and am the oldest in my family of five children. I have two younger brothers and two younger sisters. Early in my life, I knew that my parents were proud of me. I have been a hard worker on our family lands, learning early how to plow and care for the crops. I was the first of my age mates to successfully ride a donkey. I have skill on the football pitch and was the highest goal scorer for my secondary school.

Learning has come easily to me—whether planting the maize, harvesting the crops or following animal tracks. In school, I have excelled in math, science, and English. My parents depend on me, not only to behave well, but to help train and discipline my younger siblings. I have applied myself to my studies every year through Form 5 and I have always achieved one of the best grades in my class. Even when I left school for planting and harvest season, I caught up quickly. I won much recognition at Prize Giving Day. I have always had my sights set on going to the University of Botswana and I worked hard to get test scores that allow me to be in this classroom today. I am very proud to be a member of the first-year class.

When he finished, he wondered if the narrative was too self-praising, even though it was all true. He had thought about putting some other issues into the paper, but decided not to because he thought some things were not too flattering. He had enjoyed his friends, both boys and girls in secondary school. Many of his female high school classmates had admired him and sought him as a potential boyfriend. While he liked these girls, he was always too busy learning, playing sports and working the lands to give them much of a chance. He certainly did not want to stand up in front of class and say that he has never had a girlfriend. They might even think he was a homosexual!

His religious faith was another issue he chose not to write about, even though it was good to be a Christian in Botswana. Along with the rest of his family, he had regularly attended services at the Church of the Divine Light—a congregation that preached, among other things, sexual abstinence for all youth. In reality, Tsiamo did not understand much about sex beyond the basic mechanics which he studied in biology class. He knew that he was supposed to be abstinent until he was married, and that seemed a long way off. He wanted to remain abstinent, but didn't want to tell that to the whole class.

# CHAPTER 3

## Gaborone, Block 7, 5:30 AM the next day

KEFENTSE SLOWLY AWAKENED. It was early and the sun had not yet risen. She lay there knowing that she was still sleepy, but should get up anyway.

She remembered the lengthy time last evening when she had been thinking about her early life. Although parts were painful, she had found it oddly comforting to put events in order and to try to make sense out of things. She let herself lie in bed for a while and picked up her thoughts where she had left off . . .

*It was October 1995 and Gape was very excited to meet Kefentse and give her the good news. "I've got a job. I'm going to be working in the diamond mines in Letlhakane, where your brother works. He has told me how great it is to have money in your pocket. I know you and I won't be able to be together as much as we have been, but when I come home we will be able to do nice things. I can buy you fancy dresses and jewelry. This is my big chance."*

*Kefentse wasn't at all sure how she felt about this announcement. She knew it was a good thing for him and maybe it would even be a good thing for the two of them. Kefentse thought if they were to be together, Gape would have to have a job to support her. He was 18, and it was good to begin working. She would just have to learn to live with the separations.*

*Even before his announcement, Kefentse had been having day dreams about Gape in which he was kissing her. In these dreams, he was holding her in his arms and stroking her hair. He was tender and gentle, telling her how beautiful she was. In her dreams, she could see that he was very happy as he looked at her, and that made her feel good inside. When an outside noise or a voice would break the spell of her thoughts, she would realize that she had been smiling and was very, very happy. Now, knowing that she would not see him for months at a time, Kefentse was concerned. She found that her happy day dreams were gone and were replaced by worries. What if he found another girl in Letlhakane who was prettier or more fun? She thought she loved Gape and that he loved her, but nonetheless her confidence was shaken. She did not know how to stop worrying. She kept thinking she might lose him.*

*Over the next several weeks, as Gape waited for his job to begin, their meetings under the tree became more and more romantic. They would kiss with their lips closed, then began kissing with lips open as their tongues touched. She didn't know why they did this; they just did. Gape became bolder and began to touch her breasts—first through her blouse then caressing her skin. Kefentse did not know if this was right for her to allow. It was all so confusing—it felt good when he touched her, but she was also aware of the lesson of the blue bowl and what nkukuagwe had said. She would let him touch her briefly then pull his hands away, and he would stop.*

*The day before he was to leave for Letlhakane, they were sitting under the same Mokopi tree, their special place. He began to kiss her more passionately than he ever had before. It felt so right and natural to her that she just fell into a day dream as he touched her. She half-heartedly pulled his hands away, but he kept kissing and caressing her breasts. Suddenly he was touching her "down there." She both wanted him to stop and not to stop at the same time. He quickly pulled her skirt up and took off her underpants. He began pulling off his pants, and was on top of her. She wanted to say STOP, but his mouth covered hers with kisses. Gape kept saying, "Oh Kefentse, I love you so much." She didn't know what to do. She was afraid and excited at the same time, so she just let him do whatever he was going to do.*

*In a few brief minutes it was over. It hurt a little bit, but not too much. He grunted and rolled off her. What had just happened? Had they just had sex? Is that all there was to it? What did this mean? It wasn't really bad, but it wasn't particularly special either. Gape seemed to be satisfied, and that at least, made her happy. They hardly spoke as they quickly dressed and walked back to the village in silence.*

# CHAPTER 4

## Letlhakane Diamond Mine, Day 1

GAPE SAT NERVOUSLY on the combi as it rolled through the security gate of the mine. Everyone had to step out to have their O Mang carefully checked. He knew that security in the mines was always very tight. Although nervous, he felt good that he had worn his best black pants and yellow shirt and looked like an upstanding young man. Most of all he was pleased with the new black belt that his mother had bought him in Maun as a going away gift. It had a bright shiny buckle which glinted in the sun. He noted that some of the other workers were dressed shabbily. For a minute he worried that if they had to go to work immediately, he would have to do so in his good clothes. But instead, they were all taken to a room, given some preliminary instructions, and then shown to their sleeping quarters. He would be rooming with an older, more experienced miner from Orapa named Letshwenyo. Gape unpacked his few belongings, carefully placed his new belt at the bottom of a drawer and put on other clothes. He noticed that his old belt was almost worn through and he knew that it would soon break. He felt good that he had the new one as a back-up.

He and his roommate Letshwenyo went to the recreation room. They played a couple of games of pool, but Gape lost every one. Letshwenyo was a lot better at pool . . . Gape wondered if his new roommate was better at everything.

Gape had been working now for several weeks. Right from the beginning, some of the older workers had begun to tell stories about the enjoyment when drinking at the bar and bragging about having sex with girls in the village. Gape knew that he wasn't very sexually experienced, having had sex only once with Kefentse. Initially he just listened to this male banter and laughed as if he knew what they were talking about. He knew he could not reveal his lack of sexual experience—he had already shown that he was not a good pool player. On one occasion he even made up a story about a sexual encounter which had never really happened.

For a while, when lunch was over and he returned to work, he found himself thinking about Kefentse and at times would get an erection. It occurred to him that he should wait until he returned to Rakops and Kefentse before he had sex again. Soon though, other thoughts crowded this one out. He said to himself, "I am a normal 18-year-old and I have sexual needs. He wanted to be "like the rest of the guys." Just because she was the first didn't mean that she should be his only woman, and he had never promised her anything exclusive. He began to fantasize about some of the women he might meet here in Letlhakane.

Gape finished his last 7-day shift for the month and got paid. He finally had some free time and spending money. Letshwenyo and several of the other miners were going out to "get a few beers" and invited him along. Gape had not been much of a drinker in Rakops, but now he knew that nights of drinking were pretty common for the mining crew. He wanted to show that he was a man and could hold his liquor. He put on his good pants and shirt. He even celebrated by wearing his new belt with the shiny buckle. He wanted to look good for the girls who might be hanging out at the bar. As he dressed, his mind went briefly to Kefentse, but she seemed like a distant memory now. After all, she was far away and he would not see her for several months.

After his third beer at the bar, Gape began to feel light-headed and found himself laughing loudly at anyone's funny story, even if it wasn't so funny. He had noticed some of the girls in the bar who were dressed in short, tight skirts and blouses that showed a lot of cleavage. He wanted to go over and say hello, but he was still shy. The beer was helping him relax so he had another. He downed the beer in two swallows and stood for a few minutes gathering his courage. He decided he was ready to introduce himself to two of the girls who were standing at the end of the bar. Not realizing how drunk he had become, he turned quickly, lost his balance and fell flat on his face, sliding on the floor. Letshwenyo and several others started to laugh and he felt the whole bar was looking at him. Humiliated, he abandoned his plan to talk to the girls, got up and walked out of the bar without a word. The rest of the evening was a blur and he wasn't quite sure how he got back to his bed.

The next morning he found he was still sleeping in the clothes that he had worn the night before. He felt miserable . . . sick with an ache in his head. He slowly tugged off his clothes and saw that his new buckle was all scratched. He was foggy and could not figure out what happened. Then in a flash, the fall onto the bar floor came back to him in a humiliating rush. He decided the scratches on the buckle must have happened then. Slowly, he put on his work clothes including his old belt and headed off for his shift.

# CHAPTER 5

## University of Botswana Years 1-3

IT TOOK A few months for him to feel comfortable, but Tsiamo found that he could keep up well in the classroom and got excellent grades right from the very beginning. He was chosen to be on the University football team and by his second year he was a member of the starting eleven. Over time, he became interested in his female classmates and spent time with several of them. It was hard as he got older, but for the first two years, he maintained his virginity as he had been taught.

It was 1998 and the AIDS epidemic had begun to rage in Botswana and all of Southern Africa. Like many of his age mates however, Tsiamo did not pay much attention to the news. They were within the University and they felt somehow that would protect them. The students were clean, smart, successful, young people from good homes who would never be caught with "that dirty HIV disease." He knew that AIDS could be spread by having sex with someone who had the HIV virus, but many of the students said that HIV only happened to poor, unclean and ignorant persons. Besides, Tsiamo felt unstoppable. Nothing could ever harm him. He was a strong, vigorous 20 year-old man who felt he could conquer the world.

Although he was not proud of the fact, Tsiamo stopped going to church soon after he began at University. There were many devoutly religious students at UB, but also there were also many who had lived another lifestyle that included late-night parties, drinking and sex. As his church participation dropped off, the "abstinence before marriage" idea started to sound old-fashioned to Tsiamo, especially when living around all the other students who seemed not to heed that advice. When he was not in football season, parties and drinking became common for him.

In his third year, after a party where he had had a few too many beers, he had his first sexual experience with a female classmate from Mochudi. He was anxious and awkward, not knowing what this girl expected of him. He knew that to avoid a sexually transmitted illness, it was best to use a condom during sex. Tsiamo hadn't planned on having sex that evening and didn't have one with him. He was not totally sure he would know how to use it correctly anyway. This girl looked healthy and seemed eager to be sexually involved with him, so he soon forgot about the condom when they began kissing and taking off their clothes. The sex was quick but pleasurable and he left her room shortly after they finished.

The next day he began to be preoccupied with whether this girl had become pregnant. The health classes that he had attended in senior secondary school were now a distant memory. He still was not sure when a girl was most likely to become pregnant, but it made little difference now. The deed had been done and neither of them had brought up the issue.

The worry persisted and intensified for several weeks. He continued to see the same girl in class and talk with her, but he thought she looked less attractive and appealing than she had that night of the party. Nonetheless, he found his penis getting hard when he was around her. This sexual response was tempered though, by his ever-increasing fear that he would be responsible for a baby and have to drop out of school. He never raised the issue with her because pregnancy was just something that students didn't talk about. He would be too embarrassed.

Tsiamo had lunch several times with this girl and he thought he probably would like to have sex with her again, but he was afraid. The girl never mentioned anything about being pregnant, and didn't appear to be developing a bump in her abdomen. After a few months, he gradually breathed a sigh of relief and put the worry at the back of his mind. He knew he needed to know more about pregnancy before having sex again, but it was football season, and other things were more important right now.

# CHAPTER 6

## Gaborone Block 7, 6:30 AM

KEFENTSE HEARD SOME noise from the other bedroom and knew the children were stirring. The day was starting and she needed to get up. Her 16 year old, Kagiso, was her usual silent self as she bathed, dressed, ate a bit and went off to school. Dealing with Kagiso could wait until the afternoon. Bopelo, her 10 year old son was always slow to wake and needed to be prodded to dress and get off to school.

"What is a typewriter?" he asked as he ate breakfast.

"It is a machine that people use to write letters and messages when you don't use a pencil. Why do you ask?" Kefentse replied.

"Oh, they talked about it in school and said we would probably need to use one to get a good job with the government when we grow up."

Bopelo was such a sweet child. He kept his Mother on her toes with his constant and varied conversations. Today, he said no more and left the house just before the siren, the signal for school beginning. He would probably be late again and risk punishment.

Keitumetse, the youngest whom they called Ntume, was still asleep and Kefentse decided to let her stay in bed.

With Ntume asleep and the other two children gone to school, Kefentse found herself daydreaming again. She was glad to have some time to herself and her own thoughts. Times like this were rare for a mother of three children. She knew exactly where she had finished while she was lying in bed—she had had sex with Gape just as he was leaving for the mines. She knew the next few memories were not going to be pleasant, but she was determined to remember it all, just as it happened . . .

*She had become sick again and for the fourth morning in a row, she vomited. Maybe it was just a bad flu, she thought. Her breasts had begun to be sore and tender. She just felt "different," but couldn't really describe it other than the fact that she was very tired and sick at her stomach. Dintle heard her vomiting and decided that they ought to go to the clinic. The wait in the queue was long and hot—after all it was now December. Kefentse was finally seen by the nurse. After telling her about the vomiting and fatigue, the nurse examined her and asked "When was the last time you had your monthly bleeding?" Kefentse had never kept track, but now that the nurse was asking, she thought it was around the time of the Botswana Independence holiday at the end of September, a few weeks before Gape left.*

*"Have you slept with a boy?"*

*"I didn't sleep with him."*

*"I mean—have you had sex?"*

*Kefentse still wasn't quite sure what the answer was, but said, "I guess so, but only once and it was very quick"*

*"Once is enough," replied the nurse. "You are going to have a baby."*

*The reaction to Kefentse being pregnant was mixed. Her father was quite pleased at the thought of having his first grandchild and told her, "Your Mother would have been very excited." However he also quickly focused on the father of the baby. After Kefentse told him that Gape was the father, arrangements were made for Kefentse's Uncle Mpho, the brother to her mother and Uncle Lame, the brother to her father, to visit Gape's elders on the other side of the village.*

*Uncle Lame set the meeting for a Saturday at which time he and Mpho met with Gape's two Uncles, the brothers of Gape's mother. After the formal greetings, Kefentse's uncles asked what Gape's intentions were now that he was fathering a child by Kefentse. Gape's uncles were prepared for the question. "We have contacted Gape and discussed this situation with him. He admits to having laid with Kefentse once. He says that Kefentse is a good girl who has been with no other man. He is willing to take some responsibility for this baby and has asked us to give to you money to take care of Kefentse's medical care now that the baby is on the way." Kefentse's uncles quietly conferred between themselves and suggested an amount to which Gape's Uncle's agreed.*

"What are Gape's intention after the baby comes?" asked Mpho.

"Gape is hoping that he can make enough money at the mines to support Kefentse and the baby. He is a responsible boy and will send money to Kefentse every month." Kefentse's uncles were satisfied with this arrangement, accepted the money offered in the transaction and left knowing that Gape's elders would put the plan in place.

Kefentse was so excited to talk with Gape about how they were going to become a family. Unfortunately he wasn't due back in Rakops for another three weeks. He had been working at the mines for several months now and with the holidays coming up, he was going to return home for the first time. When the day finally arrived and he got off the bus, she was waiting for him. They threw their arms around each other. She wanted to discuss the baby right away, but thought it best to wait until he had time to go home, see his family and get rested. They agreed to meet later that day and go out to their "special" tree.

Later that afternoon sitting in the shadow of the tree, she said, "Gape, I am so happy to be having your baby. Even though we didn't really expect it or plan for it, now that it is happening, it is the beginning of our life together. It will be wonderful!"

Gape didn't have the overjoyed reaction that Kefentse expected. "Uh . . . yes our elders have worked out the arrangements. Uh . . . this is wonderful. I am very happy for . . . us. I will send some money from my job at the mine." As they talked more, it seemed that Gape was not interested in discussing the baby and being together as a family. He was more interested in having sex again with Kefentse. When he began caressing her and started to remove her clothes to "do it" again, she said, "No. It might hurt the baby and I can't do anything to allow that to happen. I want to do it again too, but we are just going to have to wait. My girlfriends told me that if we had sex now, I might lose the baby."

"Are you sure about that? There are guys at the mine who have had sex with pregnant girls and nothing happened." Kefentse stayed firm in her refusal and besides, she didn't want to hear about guys having sex in Letlhakane. She didn't want to think that Gape could be one of them.

They met several times more while he was home, but to Kefentse, Gape seemed cool and distant, and she didn't know why. She tried to talk about plans for the future, but he always changed the subject. He was more interested in talking about the other guys that he had met and the work that he was doing. She was glad that he didn't try to have sex again. She was determined to do everything she could to protect their baby. When he left, they agreed to write letters to stay connected.

# CHAPTER 7

## Letlhakane Diamond Mine, Month 4

GAPE WAS BACK in Letlhakane after the holidays. He and Letshwenyo would often talk when working on the same shift or if they were both off together. One day they attended an educational meeting that the company had set up for the workers about HIV/AIDS. Gape had listened to the presentations with the other miners but still had questions in his mind. He didn't speak up because he didn't want anyone to think he was ignorant. The next morning, Gape and Letshwenyo were dressing for their shift. Along with his work clothes, Gape pulled on his old belt. It snapped into two pieces. It was nothing he hadn't been expecting and besides he had his new belt as a backup. He put it on as he talked with Letshwenyo.

"Hey Letshwenyo, what do you think about this HIV thing?"

"They have been giving us these classes for a while now, but I'm not even sure it's real. You know what AIDS stands for?"

"I can't remember the words exactly, but that guy in the meeting said it was Acquired Deficiency syndrome or something like that."

"Nyaa. It means American Invention to Discourage Sex."

Gape laughed. "But why would they be teaching all this stuff if it wasn't real. It sounds scary."

"Oh I don't know; maybe there is some truth in it. I just think they are exaggerating it and trying to scare us. Even if it is a real disease, we are not going to get it. We are strong guys and that will protect us. Besides you know as well as I do that people get sick because their ancestors have done something to make the spirits angry. I come from a good family, so

I am not one to get it. It's going to be more of a problem for those dirty Zimbabweans or those from Zambia. They still live like savages while Botswana is moving ahead."

"I'm glad to hear that because I am really ready to have sex soon. I know you been with a lot of girls in this town. Give me a little advice on what to expect here."

"There are three kinds of girls. The first are the girls who were born and raised in this village. Maybe you can get them into bed but they want a husband and a family. They're not interested in just having sex."

"I don't want another one of those girls. I've already got one who thinks that way back in Rakops. I want somebody with no strings attached."

Letshwenyo seemed to puff out his chest. "Then you want one of the other two types, the sex workers and the girls who are just looking for presents. The sex workers are the easiest. As a matter of fact they will probably try to find you. As long as you are willing to pay them, the sex is easy and there are no commitments."

"That guy yesterday said we should always use a condom."

"Real men don't use condoms. Skin to skin is the only way to go. That's the way I like it."

Gape tried to sound and look just as experienced as Letshwenyo, "So what is the last type?"

"They are the type who will have sex when you give them gifts. They don't think they're sex workers. They just want what they want and will trade their bodies to get it. Sometimes they say they're looking for a 'Food Minister', a 'Minister of Fashion' or a 'Jeweler.' They will get into bed with you if you give them groceries, clothes, jewelry or other stuff. As long as you keep giving them the gifts, they are available."

"How do I tell one type from the other?"

Letshwenyo grinned, "You can tell. The girls who want a relationship don't go to bars, they go to church. The girls who hang out in the bars are hunting for a guy with money in his pocket from the mines. Once you tell them that you are looking for a good time, they will usually tell you real fast what they want in exchange—money or gifts."

"You going to the bar on Saturday?"

"Yeah I'm off"

"Okay. Let's go together I've got to get me some female pleasure."

"Yeah. By the way, the boss says they are delivering some crates with new equipment this morning and he wants us to carry them into the storage shed first thing."

"Sure let's do it now before the day gets hot."

When the crates were delivered, they began lifting and carrying them inside the storage shed. They were wooden and very heavy, but Gape was getting strong from the constant physical labor and matched Letshwenyo crate for crate. As Gape lowered the last one to the ground, he heard the scraping sound of metal on metal. He looked down to see that a nail was sticking out of the crate and that it had put a big gash in his silver belt buckle.

"The first day I wear this new belt to work, it gets scraped. Bad."

Letshwenyo was laughing, "Don't worry brother. You're still a pretty boy and you are going to get your share of female action. It's not what you have on the outside of your pants that counts. It's what you got on the inside that's important. That and how you use it. You just need some sex and Letshwenyo will take care of you on Saturday."

That weekend they showed up at the bar and as always, began downing their beers fast. After he started to feel the alcohol, Gape asked "Letshwenyo, what about that girl in the tight pink sweater at the table over there? She keeps giving me the eye and she is really good looking."

Letshwenyo grunted. "Nyaa. Forget about her. She wants a Minister of Transport and will only end up with guys like the managers who have cars. You will have better luck with those two sitting in the corner. They are straight sex workers and just want the right payment. I've done it with both of them and my former roommate did too. Just pick your favorite and go for it."

Gape did just that. Picking the shorter haired girl, they went outside for quick sex behind the building. For a second, he thought about what the educator had said during the meeting that week about using a condom.

But he liked Letshwenyo's opinion better and quickly forgot about that. He paid the extra amount that she asked for skin to skin sex, so she didn't insist on a condom either. He felt satisfied sexually, and proud that he was proving his manhood to Letshwenyo and the rest of the guys in camp.

This started what became a regular activity for Gape. He got paid at the end of the month and would send some money to Kefentse according to his Uncles' arrangement. With the rest of the money, he would go to the bar, have too many drinks and have sex with one of the girls he found there. Sometimes it was someone he had been with before and other times it was with someone who was new to town. A couple of times, when he was really interested in a girl, he would manage to buy the present that she wanted. Most of the time though, it was much easier just to pay cash.

# CHAPTER 8

## Gaborone, Block 7, 8:00 AM

KEFENTSE BROKE OUT of her daydreaming. Ntume was still not up, but this was not altogether unusual, so she took this pleasant time to continue her memories . . .

*The months skipped by and Kefentse wrote to Gape every week. But no letters came back. She knew something was wrong and her worry became worse with each passing day that she did not hear from him. She was brokenhearted. "Why doesn't he write? Isn't he excited about me and his baby? We had sex. Doesn't that mean something to him?" The more time that passed without hearing from him, the more upset and sad Kefentse became. He was leaving her.*

*For reasons that she did not understand, she began to think more about the time when her mother died. It was almost six years ago now, but the feelings seemed to come up as if it happened yesterday. She had been left and abandoned then, and she was being left and abandoned now. When she did get some news from her brother at the mines, he never talked about what Gape was doing. It was clear that something was terribly wrong. Her brother avoided talking about Gape at all.*

*When she finally heard that Gape planned to visit Rakops in May, Kefentse wasn't sure whether to be at the bus station to meet him. Eventually she decided to go, somehow hoping that things would be better than the last time. She was eight months pregnant now and heavy with child. Her ankles and face were puffy and she was afraid that she didn't look very pretty.*

*She felt nervous as Gape got off the bus. He saw her and gave her a very brief hug. It was more like he was hugging his Auntie, not the mother of his child. "How is your baby coming along? You will have to let me know whether* it's a boy or a girl. If it is a boy, I think you should call him Gape like me. It is really nice for you to meet me at the bus stop, but I have to go see my family now. Some of my friends in the neighborhood want to go out. Maybe we can get together in a couple of days. I will let you know. Besides, I have not been feeling very well these last few weeks. I think I have the flu or something. I need to rest a little."

In the pit of her stomach, Kefentse now knew that her worst fears were confirmed. She was even more heart-broken than before. He was not interested in her and not interested in the baby. He had called it "her" baby not "their" baby. She felt humiliated at having come to the bus stop. Thoughts rolled over and over in her mind—they were the same ones she had been thinking for months. What had she done? What was it that she had not done? Did he leave her because she wouldn't have sex with him again while she was pregnant? Had he found someone else? What was wrong with him? He looked thin and sick. The painful reality hit her like a flash of lightening. She was going to have to raise this baby alone. Maybe her family could help, but Gape would have no part in it.

They never did get together during the week that he was home. Several times she saw him at a distance across the road. Her heart ached, but now it was colored with anger and resentment. In her mind, she wanted to go over and pound him with her fists. "Why don't you want me now? This is our baby. Doesn't that mean something to you?" She knew she would not cause a scene and actually hit him. She had not been raised that way. She was not at the bus rank when he left for Letlhakane.

Because there was no hospital in Rakops, as her time drew near, Kefentse went to Molepolole to stay with nkukuagwe and oldest cousin Lorato. Kefentse was in a sitting room chair when the labor pains began. She called nkukuagwe who sat with her. Although at first slow and far apart, the pains intensified over several hours, but they were still not regular. The contractions were the strongest pains she had ever felt. At times, she didn't know if she could stand it any longer, but just when she felt that she might give up, they would ease off. Once in a while between pains, she cursed Gape for getting her pregnant.

*But she also longed to have him with her. If only he were willing to be a part of this and wanted to be with her, it would be easier.*

*Kefentse was admitted to the local hospital where the contractions became regular. Just when she thought they could get no worse, they did. Finally, with one last push, it was over. There she was—a beautiful baby girl—perfect in every way. Kefentse had already known what she would call her, "Kagiso—Peace." She had always thought this a beautiful name, but even more so, she hoped that this baby girl would have more peace in her life than she, Kefentse, had known. The new mother made a silent promise that she would never leave this child. She would always be there for Kagiso and help her in every way possible, even if she had to do it alone.*

*She didn't know exactly how or when it started, but it was probably a few days after Kagiso was born that Kefentse began to feel sad and cry. This was supposed to be a blessed event. Why was she crying? She was tired to her very bones. It took all her strength just to get off the couch and lift Kagiso to her breast. More bothersome, it seemed to be getting worse each day. Nkukuagwe told her this was common. "Many women feel tired and sad in the first week or two after the baby comes. Don't worry." As it had been in Botswana for generations, the mosadi mogolo closely watched over the new mother and baby daughter. By custom, there was a confinement of mother and child. Nkukuagwe determined who could visit and kept all men out. She ensured that Kefentse slept on her belly and fed her soft porridge. Gape was given news of the baby but he did not make any contact with Kefentse or her family.*

*Kefentse was not getting much sleep and thought maybe this was the reason she felt so bad. But the sadness went on and on, and seemed to be getting worse and worse. Kefentse didn't even seem pleased to have Kagiso. It was not at all like she expected. She was supposed to be happy to have a baby, but she felt empty—almost nothing at all. She wanted to feel close to Kagiso, to hold her, rock her, feed and caress her, but it felt more like something she <u>had</u> to do, not something she <u>wanted</u> to do*

*At one point, the thought crossed Kefentse's mind that if she felt so bad maybe she should kill herself. This terrified her. She had never thought of taking her own life, even when her Mother died. She also decided that she could not tell anyone about this horrible thought, not even nkukuagwe. She would have to manage on her own and she forced herself to push the horror out of her mind. She could never leave Kagiso without a mother. She knew how terrible that had been for her.*

*For the first few months, Kefentse's grandmother did everything that a traditional Botswana mosadi mogolo would do for a new mother. She cooked, cleaned, helped with the baby and greeted the visiting female guests. Eventually though, everyone could see it was taking a heavy toll on the old lady.*

*Meanwhile, Kefentse's mood was getting no better and her crying increased. Food had no appeal and despite everyone's encouragement, Kefentse did not eat. Even when nkukuagwe attended the baby, Kefentse could not rest despite feeling exhausted. She could not fall asleep. Her arms and legs felt like stone and she could barely lift them. Everyone in the family was worried about this situation. Nkukuagwe was tiring, Gape was absent and Kefentse seemed miserable.*

*Kefentse's father, hearing this news in Rakops, was worried that his daughter was not emotionally well. He was a male and didn't know much about women's things, but he knew that she was not acting like a normal new mother. What could he do? Kefentse's Mother had never been like this.*

*Kefentse became more and more panicked at the thought of leaving nkukuagwe and returning to Rakops. Nkukuagwe had become a source of strength that Kefentse depended upon and the thought of leaving her made Kefentse feel even more helpless and frightened.*

*About a week before Kefentse was to return home, her father came to Molepolole to speak with nkukuagwe. Outside of Kefentse's hearing, they discussed the situation and a phone call to Gaborone was placed. Later that day, they announced a decision. Kefentse would go to Gaborone with her Aunt Naledi for rest and support. Naledi was a younger, stronger woman and a mother herself. In truth, Naledi had always been Kefentse's favorite relative and Naledi had been eager to help when she heard of Kefentse's distress. Naledi would take Kefentse into her home until she felt better. Nkukuagwe would still oversee the progress from Molepolole and would visit regularly. Dintle and Refilwe would look after her father and the house in Rakops.*

*When told this plan, Kefentse was not sure how she felt about the decision. She did not want to leave Molepolole, but nkukuagwe was becoming more frail as time passed and the thought of being in Rakops without an adult to help her was overwhelming. It was comforting to think that she would have her Aunt to depend on, even if it meant staying in a big, strange city.*

# CHAPTER 9

## Gaborone Block 7, 8:45 AM

NTUME WALKED INTO Kefentse's bedroom wiping the sleep from her eyes. She wanted something to eat. Kefentse fixed some soft porridge, drew Ntume's bath, helped her dress and let her play in the yard. Kefentse was anxious to get back to reviewing her life and slumped into her favorite sitting room chair. Although she knew that the laundry needed doing, she didn't feel like washing the clothes. She wanted to think about her life. It was quiet in the house and the neighborhood, making it easier for her to remember and daydream . . .

*Everything was new and different in Gaborone. Kefentse had visited twice before, but not as a young mother with a new baby. The noises, the smells, the traffic; all were bothersome. She cried frequently, and kept hoping that when Kagiso slept through the night she would feel better. The days turned into weeks and then several months. Gradually, when Kagiso slept regularly and began to smile, Kefentse noticed her mood improving. Her fatigue was better and she was less prone to tears.*

*As she felt better, Kefentse realized that she liked being a new mother. She enjoyed being around her Aunt and consulted her about Kagiso's care and growth. One of Naladi's children, 21 year old Mary, had not been able to find work and was home full-time. When Naledi was at work, Mary was able to help Kefentse. With everyone's help, Kefentse even began to feel that she could successfully raise Kagiso without Gape. She felt she was coming out of a painful fog that she had been in for months.*

*As Kefentse's outlook improved, she remembered her long-held dreams of wanting to live in a big city. If her father approved, she began to think that she* would like to live in Gaborone permanently. Now that her own children were grown, Aunt Naledi seemed to enjoy having a baby in her home again,. She had always been fond of Kefentse and now Kagiso as well. Naledi could take them both of them under her wing.

When Kagiso was eight months old, Kefentse decided it was time for her and Kagiso to make a trip back to Rakops to visit her father and brothers. She also decided that it would be a time when she would ask her father if she could stay in Gaborone, find work and raise her child. Although the bus trip was long, dusty and tiring, Kefentse was excited to return with Kagiso. When she arrived with the baby, Kefentse enjoyed the attention that her father and the rest of the family showed them. The visit went well and had a beautiful conclusion when Kefentse asked her father about staying in Gaborone. He said that it would be difficult not to have regular contact with her and Kagiso, but that he could see how well Kefentse was doing now that she was staying with her Aunt. He agreed to the plan.

Being in Rakops also brought pangs of loneliness and Kefentse again found herself missing Gape. She finally gathered her courage and asked a girlfriend if Gape had been back and whether he asked about her. Her friend said that he had been back once. He knew that his child was a girl and that Kefentse was staying with her Aunt in Gaborone, but he had asked no more about them. Almost offhandedly, the friend also said, "Gape must be working very hard at the mines, because he is very thin." Kefentse remembered that Gape seemed to have lost weight the last time she saw him.

# CHAPTER 10

## Letlhakane Diamond Mine: 1 Year Later

GAPE WAS FEELING pleased with himself. He had a job and was earning a regular paycheck. Whenever he could, he went into the bar and drank as many beers as he could hold, which by this time was many more than when he first arrived in Letlhlakane. He was now a "regular" on the mining team and in the bar. People knew him and he believed that they gave him respect. He was even able to start giving advice to some of the newly hired miners. He had enough money to occasionally buy himself a new shirt or pair of pants. His belt was still quite serviceable even though the silver buckle had lost all its shine and now was grimy, dented and scratched. He regularly visited sex workers at the bar and in town. When he had money to get gifts for them, he also had sex with some of the other girls he especially liked.

For the last couple of weeks though, he had not been feeling well. He actually had stopped going to the bar and just stayed in his room at the camp. He didn't know what was wrong, but he didn't spend much time thinking about his fatigue and diarrhea. He thought they would pass and in a few days, he would feel better. After a time, he did feel more like himself. He had saved some money from not going out for several nights and did some quick arithmetic. If he didn't send the full amount to Kefentse this month, he would have enough money to rent a room at the Letlhlakane Lodge and stay with a sex partner the whole night. He liked that plan and thought he could always make up the difference by paying Kefentse extra next month.

That weekend after his usual quota of beers, Gape saw a new girl walking to the bar. By this time he knew all the locals from Letlhakane, but he didn't recognize her. He assumed she was probably a sex worker from the way she dressed and flirted with all the men as soon as she came into the room. He went over and introduced himself and found that her name was Tiro. An appropriate name he thought—she was a "working girl." He negotiated a price for the whole night and went with her to the Lodge. He was feeling pretty drunk, but that didn't stop him from having sex twice before he fell sound asleep on the bed.

He awoke the next morning to find that Tiro was gone along with his wallet and the few pula he had left in it. He was initially quite angry but then began to think about the stories that other mine workers had told about thefts by sex workers. He was even able to chuckle a bit at himself. "So it finally happened to me. I guess I am not as lucky as I thought. No worries. I'm getting paid again in two weeks and I can get myself a new wallet. At least she left me my shirt and pants." He had heard one story about a miner who not only had his money stolen, but all his clothes as well. That guy had to get back to the mine in his underwear.

Aching a bit, Gape got up slowly. For the second time in a month, he had to pull the belt one notch further in to make it tight. He wasn't exactly sure why he was losing weight but he figured it was due to the long hours of work in the hot sun. As he walked to the place where he would hitchhike back to the mine, he noticed that he again started to feel somewhat bad. He wasn't sick to his stomach, but he just felt weak and tired. He couldn't quite understand it. He thought he should be building muscles doing heavy mine work, but he felt weaker and weaker. As before, he did not think too much about it and knew he could go to the company doctor if it got worse.

In fact, the tiredness did not get better. That night he had to tell the boss that he was sick and would visit the doctor in the morning. He missed a second day of work before he eventually got back on the job, but he still felt that he was only working at half speed.

# CHAPTER 11

## Gaborone, Block 7, 10 AM

Feeling hungry, Kefentse left the sitting room chair and went to the kitchen. There was one fat cake left on the counter and she munched on it as she made her way back to the stuffed chair. She remembered where she had left off in her thoughts. "I had just come to Gaborone to stay . . .

*Now that she was staying full time with Naledi in Gaborone, she had begun to think about her future and that of Kagiso. Part of her wanted to stay in her Aunt's home and simply be a mother. But another part of her knew that in order to stay here, she would have to work to earn money. Her cousin Mary was not working and could help care for Kagiso. But what job could she get? What could she do? Because of Kagiso's birth, Kefentse had not finished secondary school and was not qualified to do much of anything . . . maybe cook, clean, and take care of a household. Kefentse discussed this with her Aunt. Naledi knew that Kefentse was too smart not to complete her education. The family might need to sacrifice for a time without an added income, but Naledi suggested, and Kefentse happily agreed, that the best thing was for Kefentse to return to school and earn her certificate.*

*The next two years were hard for Kefentse. She was a full-time student at the local senior secondary school and a mother to Kagiso. But she managed. She found the teachers in Gaborone very interested in learning and education. This was particularly true of Mma Moremi, her English teacher. Mma Moremi was always encouraging and quickly noticed Kefentse's interest in reading. Despite her many obligations, Kefentse found time to do the extra reading assignments that Mma Moremi would give her. Her reading skills improved rapidly, and she read everything that she could find, pleased to feel that she was becoming a learned young woman.*

*Kagiso was changing too. She had turned into a happy, healthy toddler. She had her mother's determination and good looks. Kefentse felt very lucky to have Mary available during the day to care for the baby. Even with this positive situation, she was very protective of Kagiso. She remembered all too clearly losing both her Mother and Gape. More than many mothers, she felt a need to protect her baby from any harm. She convinced herself that Kagiso was with family who loved her and all would be fine. So far anyway, that had been true.*

*One day in her final year of school, Kefentse's oldest brother came to visit Gaborone from Rakops. He brought very bad news about Gape. He told her that a few months before, Gape had stopped working in the mines because he had become very sick. Rumors had spread in Rakops that since being at the mines, Gape had become a wild and undisciplined young man. People said that he had been drinking heavily and was thought to have a different woman in his bed every night . . . some town girls and even sex workers. The gossip in the town was that Gape had picked up an illness in Letlhakane. He had begun missing work and was eventually fired. He came back to the village and those who knew him were shocked at his appearance. He was painfully thin, weak and pale, and never did regain his strength. No one would speak of what actually caused his sickness, but his health deteriorated rapidly and he died two months after returning home.*

*Kefentse was shocked and saddened. Gape had been out of her life for two years now, but she still thought about him. He had gone from being a nice boy to a young man whose life had been changed by drinking and sexual excess. It had been such a horrible change. Although he had left her, she would never forget him as her first love and the father of her daughter.*

*Kefentse eventually finished Form 5. Her dream of completing school and taking her exams had come true. As she waited for her results, hoping to have earned her certificate, she began searching for work. She knew this would not be easy. Her cousin Mary had not been able to find a job for almost three years. As was her nature, Kefentse started looking immediately. She walked to all the shops and businesses in their ward, but there was no work. She was not discouraged though; it was only the first week.*

*The next morning, Kefentse had just begun looking at the newspaper adverts when Kagiso began to scream. She was not a problem child, and it was unusual for her to cry so loudly. When Kefentse picked her up, Kagiso felt warm, and looked pale. Kefentse offered her food, but she wouldn't eat and continued to cry. She hoped this was not something serious and put Kagiso down to nap, but the crying continued. Within a half hour, Kagiso felt even hotter and was listless except for her crying. Kefentse knew that something was wrong and she needed to take the baby to the clinic. She wasn't sure which clinic was closer to the house, but finally decided that it was the one toward the city center. She wrapped Kagiso in a blanket and set out for the clinic.*

*After waiting in the queue, she finally was shown to the consultation room, The nurse who examined Kagiso had a worried look on her face. "Kagiso's temperature is very high, and she obviously has some illness, but I don't know what it is just yet. Is anyone else at home sick?" Kefentse said "No" and was becoming more worried herself. The nurse said, "I will check with the Medical Officer, but I think he will want to put her in the hospital to find out what's wrong." Kefentse didn't know whether to be happy or sad about this plan. It meant that Kagiso was seriously ill, but in the hospital, she would have doctors and nurses to make sure she got better. Kefentse agreed, the doctor approved and arrangements were made for Kagiso to be admitted to the hospital.*

*Even on the Children's ward, the hospital was a scary place. Babies were lying on mattresses on the floor; some were obviously very sick. Several of the children were so thin that Kefentse didn't see how they would live even one more*

day. Other children had hollow, sunken eyes and seemed not to be interested in anything.

Eventually, a doctor came to look at Kagiso. In the middle of the exam, he left and did not return for several hours. During the wait, Kefentse talked with several other mothers who were there with their children. She asked the women why their children were in the hospital. One said that her son had pneumonia. Another said that her daughter was just growing weak and losing weight, but the doctors did not know what was wrong. "The doctor said something about HIV, but I don't believe it."

Her baby was on the same ward with someone who might have this new disease, HIV! Kefentse had been reading about the rapid spread of this fatal illness in Africa. She was suddenly terrified.

The doctor returned and finished the exam. He had the same look of concern on his face as the clinic nurse. "I need to ask you some questions." He asked" Was anyone sick at home? Had she, Kefentse been sick? Was the baby's father well?"

She answered all the questions truthfully and directly, including Gape's symptoms, illness and death. "That is a concern," the doctor murmured. "Have you or the baby ever been tested for HIV?" "No," she replied and the more they talked, the more panicked she became. Although Kefentse herself had never been sick, Gape had died of some unnamed illness.

A thought suddenly struck her like lightening! Could Gape have died of HIV? If he did, could he have passed it on to her, or even to Kagiso? If so, would she and her baby die? No, this couldn't happen. From then on, she answered the doctor's other questions, but felt in a daze. She vaguely remembered the doctor saying," We will be doing some more tests and will let you know when we have the results."

Since Kefentse was given permission to spend the night with Kagiso, the staff encouraged her to return home, gather some clothes and toiletries, and then return to the hospital. Feeling anxious and confused, she went out into the hot sun and walked home.

When she arrived home, Kefentse called Naledi in a panic, begging her to leave work and come to the house. Naledi came quickly and Kefentse broke down in tears, exploding with emotion and questions. *"Why did this happen? What is wrong with Kagiso? The doctor asked about HIV—were we tested? Was anyone else sick? I told him about how Gape died. Kagiso can't have HIV—she just can't! And I must live to be her mother."* Naledi too was worried. She tried to reassure Kefentse and agreed to go back to the hospital with her to see the baby.

Kagiso looked so helpless in her crib—weak, whimpering and still feverish. Now there was an intravenous line placed in her small foot with clear liquid passing through the tubing. Nothing else had changed. Kagiso seemed to barely recognize her mother. Kefentse was not calmed.

That night Kefentse slept little. She could only think about Kagiso, her tiny baby . . . her small and terribly sick baby. *"My little girl just can't have HIV. She's not going to die. I won't let her die, and I must stay well too. She must not lose her Mother."*

As the sun peaked through the window, she came to a conviction—she would make a promise to her God and to her ancestors. If both she and Kagiso lived, Kefentse would do everything in her power to keep her little girl safe and protected in the future. She would read and learn everything she could to be the best mother possible. She knew that she didn't know as much as she should about this terrifying illness called HIV. She vowed that when Kagiso got better—and she HAD to get better—she would do whatever it took to be the best mother she could.

Sitting with Kagiso, nothing changed and the hours seemed like weeks. The doctor was not around to give her any further information, but the nurse said that Kagiso's fever was still very high. The doctor gave the Kagiso more intravenous fluids, started an antibiotic and some medication to lower the fever. Her temperature came down only a little, but there was no real change. The next days dragged on in the same pattern . . . unendingly long hours with no apparent progress while the baby continued to be feverish and sick. Kefentse's anxiety grew daily. This was a nightmare. When would it go away? The hospital staff still had no answer for what was causing the illness.

*Day three . . . Day four . . . Day five . . . and still no improvement. Kefentse was so emotionally distraught, she could not eat, could not sleep and could barely concentrate. It was endless . . .*

*On the sixth day, the fever broke, and Kagiso's temperature rapidly decreased. She began to drink small amounts and little by little appeared to be getting better. Kefentse was overcome with relief. By the seventh day, Kagiso's temperature was normal, and she had begun to eat solid foods. She was much more lively and alert, recognized her mother and begged to be held.*

*The doctor told Kefentse that Kagiso's HIV test had been sent to the South African laboratory. It was only after the test results came back that she would know if Kagiso had the HIV virus. Because the illness had cleared so fully, the doctor was optimistic that the cause of the illness was probably a less severe infection which had run its course. Nonetheless, before she left the hospital, the doctor wanted to test Kefentse for HIV as well. He said it was a simple blood test and they would have the results of both tests in two to three weeks.*

*Mother and daughter returned home, but time passed slowly. Kefentse tried to keep herself from worrying about the test results. The more she thought about it and read material about HIV and AIDS, the more convinced she was that Gape had died of the disease. The rumors of his sex and drinking behavior fit the pattern of people who were most at risk of getting HIV. But when did he get the illness? Did he have it when they had sex? Could she have it and not know it? Even though she was now acting normally, could Kagiso still have that virus and become sick again?*

*As instructed, Kefentse went back to the clinic in three weeks. The long wait in the queue was made worse by her increasing nervousness about the test results. She finally was seated in the office and was trembling as the nurse came in.*

*"I have both of your test results here. You and Kagiso do <u>not</u> have HIV." Kefentse sank into the chair in blessed relief, only partially listening to anything else the nurse said. Her ears perked up however when the nurse mentioned Gape. "The doctor told me about the baby's father. From what you have been able to tell us about how he became sick and how he looked, he most likely did*

*have AIDS and died of it. Your negative tests indicate however that he did not pass it on to you or your baby." Again Kefentse felt a surge of relief.*

*It was only later as she walked home, that she remembered the rest of what the nurse said "Since you did not catch the virus from your sexual contact with him, it is likely that he was not infected at that time. We know now that there is a high percentage of HIV among the mine workers who are separated from their families. It could be that Gape contracted the virus by having unprotected sex when he was working there. It is a good thing that you did not have unprotected sex with him again."*

*It all came so clear to her now. If Gape had stayed with her, they would no doubt have had unprotected sex again, and she would not have known about his illness! She could have been infected—she most likely <u>would</u> have been infected. She had just been lucky. She was now even more determined to make sure that never again would she or Kagiso depend on luck to stay healthy.*

*Kefentse's Cambridge test results arrived. She missed earning her certificate by just a few points, which meant that she had to consider a future without a university degree. Devastated, Kefentse thought, "If only my mother had lived; if only I had not had to drop out of school. If only I had not had a baby so young . . . I just know I could have made it to university." She knew these were wasted thoughts however—about what might have been. She would just have to use strength and determination to face the next phase of her life. Her Aunt's family had just been scraping by with two extra mouths to feed. Kefentse had to renew her efforts to find a job. Now that Kagiso had recovered, she needed to begin looking again right away.*

*She never realized how tiring it was to apply for job after job, but receive no offers. She knew she would find something eventually, she just knew it, but the process was exhausting. Day after day, she persisted, spending most of the day looking at job adverts and applying to any open position. One month turned into into two . . . then three . . . then four.*

She had visited almost every business in the nearby areas of Gaborone, some two or three times. In each case there were no openings or when there was an opening, she was not selected. She read the newspaper, or at least part of it every day, both because she enjoyed keeping up with the news, and she could look for new job adverts. One day, she noticed a small box at the back of the *Daily News*. "Wanted: two general maintenance workers at the University of Botswana." It caught her eye immediately. Not only was it a possible job, but it was at the University, a place of learning. She tucked a copy of the *Daily News* in her purse and went to the campus that very day.

After she found the Human Relations Office, Kefentse took her place with the others in the job application queue. She was dismayed, because everyone looked older and more experienced than she. Nonetheless, she filled out the application knowing that her English skills were good and that maybe that would help her chances. When the manager came out to take her paperwork, Kefentse was reading the newspaper. "I see you like to read," the manager said. "Yes. It has always been one of my favorite things to do" Kefentse replied. The manager eyed her carefully and said "We don't always get a lot of applicants for maintenance positions who can read well. What is your name?" Kefentse told her and added "Mma, I would very much like one of these jobs. I am a hard worker, and I can be depended upon. I hope you will give me a chance to prove myself."

~·~

Three days later, the Human Relations manager offered her a job in the grounds maintenance department. Kefentse was overjoyed. It was not the kind of professional job she had hoped to have, but it was a job! She would have a salary even though it was small. She would also be able to be around smart people . . . University students and professors. As a University employee, she was also pleased to find that she would have access to the UB library. She could take out books and use the reading room when she was not working. She could barely contain her delight.

Ntume came into the room crying. "I fell down and hurt myself." Kefentse saw that it was only a scraped knee with some gravel in the cuts. She washed the wound, Ntume scampered out to play and Kefentse returned to her thoughts—now she was getting to a joyous part of her life.

# CHAPTER 12

## University of Botswana, Year 4

ONE AFTERNOON AFTER the season was finished, Tsiamo was walking back to his dorm. It happened in an instant . . . he spied a girl that made him stop in his tracks. She was the most beautiful creature he had ever seen. He was stunned and simply could not keep his eyes off her. She was wearing a worker's uniform, appeared to be doing some cleanup tasks along the school sidewalk. and he assumed she was a University employee. He wanted to start a conversation but was suddenly tongue-tied. "What if I make a fool of myself? What if I start stuttering or can't get the words out? What if she doesn't want to talk to me?" He knew he wanted to say hello, but first thought it would be best to go back to the dorm and change the old shirt he was wearing. As he walked to the room and put on fresh clothes, he couldn't keep his mind from thinking about her and seeing her beautiful face and lovely body . . .

He went back to find her, but she wasn't there. He was disappointed but determined to find her again. Tsiamo spotted another worker across the courtyard dressed in the same uniform as the girl. He asked him who the young woman worker was and learned her name was Kefentse. She had left for the day but her co-worker thought she would return tomorrow. All night, Tsiamo thought about this girl, excited and sleepless. He would find her in the morning.

After his early class, Tsiamo returned to the same area of campus where he had seen the girl the previous day, but there was no sign of her. It was a mild, sunny day and he decided to sit on a bench and wait. Opening his backpack, he removed a book and pretended to be deep in study. In fact, his eyes never stopped scanning the area, looking for that beautiful girl.

After an hour, Tsiamo was about to give up, when suddenly, there she was. She was pulling a cleaning trolley and seemed to be lost in her own thoughts. Gathering his courage, Tsiamo quickly returned the book to his pack, got up and went to her. As he approached, Tsiamo's heart began pounding against his chest . . . he felt sure that she would see it beating right through his shirt.

# CHAPTER 13

## Gaborone, Block 7, 10 AM

KEFENTSE REMEMBERED THE next scene as if it happened yesterday . . .

*She was working on the school grounds when she saw this tall, good looking Motswana student walking toward her. She looked at the face of the approaching young man and knew immediately that someone special had just stepped into her future. Somewhat shyly, he said hello, told her his name—Tsiamo. After asking her name and talking for a while, he asked if he might see her after work that afternoon. She happily said yes.*

*That was the first day of the rest of their lives.*

Kefentse and Tsiamo saw each other every day for the next three months. For the first time since that young 15 year old girl had held Gape's hand in Rakops, Kefentse felt something stir and recognized the feelings. With Tsiamo though, they came in a more wonderful way. She was older and could see that Tsiamo was a good person and an exceptional man. He was kind, caring, smart, and the sort of man she knew would be a good mate.

For his part, Tsiamo saw in Kefentse the kind of girl he'd only dreamed about. While working in a humble position, she was still proud and confident. She was intelligent, charming and challenged him to be his best.

Tsiamo and Kefentse fell deeply in love. He accepted Kagiso as his own child and within the year, the three of them were living with Naledi and had come together as a family.

Tsiamo graduated from the University Project Management program with excellent grades and immediately found a government position in the Department of Transportation. Happily for all of them, Kefentse was soon pregnant with their first child together. Their son Bopelo was born in the summer of their second year together and they were married six weeks later.

Time seemed to pass quickly for their growing family of four. They all began to attend church together. Tsiamo did well in the Department of Transportation in Gaborone. His superiors saw his potential and transferred him to a junior management position in Ramotswa three years after they were married. As Tsiamo's job responsibility increased, so did his salary. They were able to move out of Naledi's house and find a small but pleasant home of their own in Block 7. Although neither of them liked to have him commute to Ramotswa, the good salary had allowed him to buy a car and it simply meant that the workday was longer. During the sixth year of their relationship, Kefentse joyfully announced that she was again pregnant. They welcomed another daughter into the family whom they named Keitumetse, but everyone called her Ntume. The family was growing and times were good.

As he had always done, Tsiamo did whatever it took to do his job well and completely. The commute made for exhausting days though. He started having a beer or two in the evenings to relax. Even on weekends, he had less and less energy to interact with Kefentse and the children. Although he was fatigued, Tsiamo knew that hard work on the job paid off in the end. Ahead lay a rosy horizon for the five of them . . . or so they thought.

# CHAPTER 14

## University of Botswana, 4 Years Later

WHEN THERE WAS no one to sit with at lunch on campus, Kefentse read the Daily News. She saw the latest government statistics of HIV in Botswana. Almost one in every five people in her country were now HIV positive. The rate for women of child-bearing age was between thirty and forty percent. Young men and women were also being infected with other sexually transmitted illnesses. More people died from AIDS and tuberculosis than malaria, heart disease, stroke, violent deaths and car accidents put together! She had seen the billboards and watched the television shows about HIV. The news was only getting worse and more frightening to her, especially as Kagiso, her oldest, would soon reach adolescence. Kefentse saw that thousands of teenagers across the country were infected with the virus and knew all too well the vulnerabilities of being an adolescent.

After all, Kefentse herself was a perfect example of the dangers . . . she had been ignorant about relationships, sexual activity, becoming a woman and having an unplanned pregnancy. She remembered the meetings with Gape and their first and only act of intercourse at age 16, leading to her pregnancy with Kagiso. Most strongly, she remembered how Gape left soon after, breaking her heart. Having a child at such a young age had totally dictated the course of Kefentse's life. Her school progress had been interrupted by her mother's death, but it was becoming a teen parent that destroyed any future dreams of a professional career. Being a maintenance woman, particularly for the University, was not such a bad thing. It was a job that was steady and predictable. Secondly, even though she was young, she had already become an assistant supervisor through a bit of good fortune and her own talents. But still, she looked with envy upon the University students and professor as she went about her work. She knew that studying or teaching at a university though, would never be possible for her.

Of course she loved Kagiso, with all her heart. Having her, Bopelo and Ntume filled her life with joy. But still . . . she had no options. She did not want this for her children. She wanted them to have a choice. She wanted them to have everything that she never did. Kefentse wanted her children to live their dreams with all of their abilities. AIDS, however, had become extremely dangerous in Botswana. AIDS could kill. Botswana now had the second-highest AIDS rate in the world and it was still growing. Just as she had done with so many things in her life, she made a decision then and there to renew the vow she had made when Kagiso was sick. She would give her children all the available information about HIV and teach them about relationships, sex and decision making. They needed this in order to grow up safe, smart and strong. She would honor her Mother by being the kind of parent that her Mother would have been.

Where to go? Where to start? She remembered her days as a child when she read books and magazines filled with information and learning. She could read better now and knew that the library, where she could go as a University employee, was one place she could get some help. On her next day off she went to the library and began browsing through the books. She focused on those that talked about self-help, self-development, raising children, and anything she could find on teaching children about sex. There were remarkably few books for such an important topic. Her eyes fell on one called "*Power Parents*" and she began to leaf through it. The book appealed to her right away. A Power Parent was what she wanted to be and this book would show her how. She checked out the book and began to read it as soon as she got home . . .

# POWER PARENTS
# CHILDREN AND SEX

## WHO IS A POWER PARENT?

- ✓ A parent who is strong in body, mind and spirit
- ✓ A person who understands the enormous influence parents have on their children
- ✓ A parent who knows the importance of sexuality in a child's overall development
- ✓ A parent who is determined to talk about sex with his/her child, even if it is initially uncomfortable
- ✓ A parent who helps a child make smart decisions, leading to emotional growth from childhood to adolescence to adulthood
- ✓ A parent who understands the difference between Sexuality, Sensual Activities and the Sexual Act

# POWER POINTS FOR POWER PARENTS:

- **SEXUALITY, SENSUAL ACTIVITIES AND "SEX" ARE DIFFERENT THINGS.**

- **TRADITIONAL IDEAS ABOUT TALKING TO CHILDREN MUST BE RE-EVALUATED.**

- **PREVIOUSLY "TABOO" TOPICS MUST BE DISCUSSED OPENLY.**

- **PARENTAL BEHAVIOR MUST BE EXAMINED TO MEET TODAY'S REALITIES.**

## HOW TO BE A COMPETENT, INFORMED POWER PARENT

Power Parenting of course, involves knowledge about reproduction and biology. For some parents, the process begins with updating their own information. There are many books that detail the important points of anatomy of sexual organs and reproductive physiology (See Appendix 1). These can be used in addition to this text for that information.

Beyond just biological knowledge though, being a Power Parent is more about an attitude and willingness to assist your children with their emotional development, particularly as it involves sexuality, male-female relationships and partner choices. Up until now, there has been very little guidance about the nature of this approach and how to develop it. There are few, if any, guidebooks to assist parents in learning where, when and how to talk with children and teens. Where do I start? What words do I use? How do I best help my kids stay safe? Read on and this book will tell you.

A starting point is to understand the difference between sexuality, sensuality and the often misunderstood concept of "sex."

**_Sexuality_** is a part of our human nature, our gender and all that we are as a man or a woman. Sexuality is a complex part of each of us that includes both physical and psychological components. The informed parent recognizes that the expression of sexuality is influenced by culture, religious belief and family tradition. Understanding sexuality is an essential part of a child's emotional growth and development.

**_Sensual/sexual activities_** are the wide range of behavior between people including flirting, touching, physical affection, embracing, kissing, caressing, and stimulation of body parts. This stimulation includes, but is not limited to breasts as well as oral, anal and genital intercourse. The knowledgeable parent knows that sexual activity combines biological, physical and emotional aspects. The biological desire to reproduce is combined with the body's arousal. When aroused, there is a physical response of the body and the emotional bonds between sexual partners are created.

*"__Sex__"* is often assumed to be to be limited to the physical activity of sexual intercourse. The Power Parent knows that "sex" includes intercourse plus many sensual activities which have both physical and emotional aspects.

## CHARACTERISTICS OF A POWER PARENT:

## A BOTSWANA POWER PARENT:

- ✓ Understands the tremendous cultural and economic changes in Botswana over the last five decades and recognizes how these developments affect family functioning.

- ✓ Wisely knows that child-rearing styles need to evolve to successfully cope with modern issues faced by children and their caregivers.

- ✓ Recognizes the intense burden that HIV/AIDS places on our children in the complicated process of reaching adulthood.

- ✓ Knows that being a parent requires the gradual empowerment of children to be safe and smart adults with sound decision-making skills and clear thinking.

- ✓ Knows that ignorance or inaccurate sexual knowledge places our children at risk.

- ✓ Instills moral values in a child and helps the child develop a value system of his/her own.

&#10003; Passes on to their children the best of Botswana tradition and culture.

In contemporary times, a successful parent knows both the old and the new realities of Botswana family life. Traditional Batswana ideas about child rearing are still practiced in many families and have changed little from generations ago. They are often repeated with little evaluation of whether they are appropriate, useful or effective today. Some of these long-held concepts include:

&#10003; A child should neither be seen nor heard but disciplined as needed.

&#10003; Children are talked <u>to</u>, but seldom talked <u>with.</u>

&#10003; Taboo topics and activities, including those about sex and sexuality are to be avoided or there will be "consequences." These consequences were rarely spelled out, but "something bad" can happen.

&#10003; Children are directly and indirectly given the message, "Don't talk about sex."

&#10003; If menses is discussed at all, it is a secretive thing. Don't tell anyone. A menstruating girl is to be avoided. Once menses starts, a girl is to avoid and "be careful" of being near boys. Specifics are not provided and the girl has to figure it out for herself.

&#10003; Nocturnal emissions ("wet dreams") in boys are never discussed by the mother. A father might address this, but often does not, leaving the boy to figure out for himself what is happening to him.

- ✓ If a child expresses ideas that are different from the parents, it is being disrespectful.

- ✓ Toddlers and young children of both genders are raised by mothers. Even as they become older, fathers are minimally involved with raising the children.

- ✓ Teens are not expected to develop romantic relationships. If and when such relationships develop, they are kept secret from the parents.

- ✓ Just prior to their wedding, brides are given a brief orientation to sexuality by their aunts, but often up to that time, there is little information or direction given to help girls during the important dating and courtship phases of relationships.

- ✓ Boys are told that "your cattle are your future." There is no talk about how to be a husband or father, physically or emotionally.

## REALITIES FOR MODERN PARENTS:

- ✓ Older traditions of parenting in Botswana need to be examined. New developments and problems require new approaches and solutions.

- ✓ Because of AIDS, many young parents today have lost one or both of their own parents. They were raised in either single-parent homes, by relatives or other caregivers. Often they have had little or no parental modeling when faced with raising their own family.

✓ Before completing their own development and forming solid values themselves, some teens become parents. They raise their children as best they can with limited experience to guide them.

✓ Many parents today have been raised in rural villages. But now they live in cities and face new challenges in rapidly urbanizing Botswana.

✓ Many life issues have changed significantly and quickly in Botswana—economic status, quality and availability of housing, availability of clean water, electricity, modern transport, the development and spread of cities. Unfortunately, concepts of parenting and raising children have not kept pace.

✓ At the lands, the men continue to give boys instruction on raising crops, tending herds, milking cows, riding donkeys and hunting. But they give little factual information around issues of powerful sexual drives, peer pressure and sexuality in a world filled with the possibility of life threatening illnesses.

✓ Girls continue to be taught cooking, cleaning, home management and infant care. Rarely are girls given even basic knowledge on love, evaluating potential life partners, and the emotional and physical aspects of being a sexual female. Fathers are not involved in helping girls learn about the opposite sex.

✓ Many parents today are lost. They surely want to help their children lead safe, proud, successful lives, but there have not been roadmaps available. The realities faced by their parents and grandparents in past generations are not the same as those faced by the parents in Botswana today.

Nowhere is the challenge for parents more urgent than in dealing with sexuality in the era of HIV. Even with available treatment through anti-retro viral medications (ARV's), HIV/AIDS is frightening. There remains no cure. HIV is a lifelong illness. Failing to have correct information can lead to chronic ill health, lifetime medication with significant side effects and social discrimination. Today with ARV treatment, AIDS is no longer an immediate death sentence. Life can be prolonged, but infected individuals eventually succumb to the disease or the complicating illnesses that commonly occur with HIV. These related conditions—cancer, tuberculosis, brain infections or losing the ability to think rationally and care for day-to-day needs (AIDS dementia)—can be painful and difficult for the infected person and their families. Although one can now live with HIV, the best strategies continue to be knowledge, protection and prevention. Parents are in the best position to provide all three of these measures for their children.

## WHY TALK WITH CHILDREN ABOUT SEX, SEXUAL RELATIONSHIPS AND SEXUALITY?

### POWER POINTS FOR POWER PARENTS:

- IF NOT FROM PARENTS, WHERE WILL CHILDREN LEARN ABOUT SEX?

- SMART DECISIONS DO NOT COME AUTOMATICALLY FROM GROWING OLDER, THEY COME FROM WISE COUNSEL WITH TRUSTED ELDERS

- PARENTAL INVOLVEMENT WILL HELP COUNTERACT THE DISTORTED GENDER MESSAGES SO COMMON IN THE MEDIA

It is **our duty** as adults to help our children with challenging life issues. For generations, parents have taught their children important things—avoiding the risks of wild animals, how to hunt for food and raising crops in times of drought. These teachings have been crucial to health and growth. HIV is a deadly illness that lurks in our very neighborhoods with almost 1 of every 5 Batswana being HIV positive. Isn't it even more important today to teach children about the ways to stay healthy and grow up safely?

✓ While adults and school children alike can repeat crucial facts and recommendations about HIV/AIDS, there are still roadblocks to good health, even for children who have the facts. Schools teach HIV facts as well as basic reproductive biology, but even the best classes cannot adequately prepare children for the emotional issues of sexuality. These lessons are best taught at home.

✓ In Botswana, HIV is primarily transmitted through heterosexual intercourse. Therefore the ABC's of protection—Abstinence, Be faithful, and Condomize are crucial principles that most school children have heard many times. Safe Male Circumcision, and the elimination of Multiple Concurrent Partnerships (MCP) are other ways to decrease the likelihood of contracting HIV. All of these are important building blocks of knowledge, but smart and consistent behaviors are necessary to remain HIV free. Facts and knowledge are important, but they are only one part of the solution. How we teach children to translate this knowledge into day-to-day behaviors is critical. The solid moral context which will guide smart decision-making does not happen automatically. It must be conveyed by an ongoing dialogue between parents and their children. Parents must be involved.

✓ Getting an HIV test to learn one's status is the gateway to guiding further behavior, but many of our citizens are not tested because of ignorance or fear. Younger teens cannot be HIV tested without parental or guardian consent. Many sexually active younger teens are afraid to reveal that they have a boyfriend or girlfriend to their parents, much less their sexual activity. Therefore, they do not ask for this consent. They remain ignorant about their own and their partner's status and therefore putting themselves at risk.

✓ If not from parents:

♦ Where do children learn about sexuality and a healthy self-esteem?

♦ How do they learn that smart decisions may involve saying "No" to peers and potential sexual partners?

♦ Where will children develop the self-confidence to stand up for their own beliefs effectively and consistently?

♦ Where do children learn to deal effectively with their own sexual drives and desires?

♦ How do they learn to choose responsible and safe marital/ sexual partners?

♦ How do young adults learn to identify potentially demeaning, emotionally abusive or even possibly violent partners?

♦ Where will young people come to understand the signs of physical, emotional or sexual abuse?

**Active parenting is essential in meeting today's family challenges.**

# TRUTHS ABOUT SEXUALITY

✓ Sexuality is an essential part of the human experience—It is natural and healthy. God created this for us. Without sexual activity the human race would perish.

✓ Sexual feelings are powerful. Our children need guidance to understand and deal with these feelings as they emerge.

✓ All children eventually mature into sexual beings. It is natural and expected. As concerned and informed parents, we want the expressions of sexuality to occur at the right time and in a healthy way

✓ Sexuality and interactions with the opposite gender have much to do with developing self-esteem. Talking with children about becoming a man or a woman develops their inner strength and creates positive self-image.

✓ The media—TV, magazines and movies—give distorted messages about masculinity, femininity and sexuality. The parent who is concerned about this problem makes certain to provide accurate and timely information within sound moral principles to counteract these exaggerated and unhealthy messages.

✓ When Power Parents are willing to tackle sensitive issues about sexuality, they improve overall communication with their children. By developing a sense of trust with children about sexual issues, Power Parents lay the groundwork for discussions on a wide variety of other important areas.

✓ Children/teens are less likely to take sexual risks if they have a positive view of themselves and their sexuality. This positive view comes from a gradual introduction of sexuality with age-appropriate factual knowledge and moral direction.

✓ <u>Not</u> knowing about sexuality and male-female relationships can leave our children open to emotional or physical harm, poor partner choices, contracting HIV or other sexually transmitted illnesses.

✓ Ask yourself—Where did I get sex information as a child? Was it clear, thorough and helpful? Did I get this information from my parents or another responsible adult? If I didn't get such counsel, would it have been helpful if I had? Were you able to experience an initiation rite? If you did, were all your questions answered?

**Considering all of this then, the question is not <u>should</u> we talk with children about sexuality, but <u>how</u> to do it in the most effective way. That is the purpose of this book.**

## RISKS AND ROADBLOCKS TO TALKING WITH CHILDREN AND TEENS ABOUT SEX

### POWER POINTS FOR POWER PARENTS:

- **ROADBLOCKS TO TALKING ABOUT SEX COME FROM OUTDATED IDEAS AND TRADITIONS.**

- **TALKING ABOUT SEX WITH CHILDREN <u>LOWERS</u> THE LIKELIHOOD OF SEXUAL EXPERIMENTATION AT A YOUNG AGE[1].**

---

[1] *see Appendix 2, Page 157.

Roadblocks to talking about sex with our children reside in our minds. Many parents believe that sex is a taboo subject, and at best, an uncomfortable topic to be avoided. This pattern of avoidance and silence may have been instilled in us from our own parents and their attitudes about sex. If we never experienced trusting, loving and open communication with them, how are we to know how to approach our own children? Although talking with an auntie or uncle is supported by Botswana tradition, it is less available now that many children live in cities far from their family village and extended family. Information given by these relatives is given often in analogies and metaphor. Today's parents are frequently anxious and inexperienced about sexuality themselves. Raised to believe that sex was mysterious scary and taboo, we often pass this attitude on to our children. Nothing could be less helpful!

✓ Many Botswana parents fear that talking about sex will encourage sex to occur earlier and more frequently—**THIS IS NOT TRUE.** Rather than encourage early experimentation, it has been shown repeatedly that children who talk with their parents about sex are more likely to postpone having sex[2].

✓ Whether a discussion is about a positive or negative activity, communication does not cause a child to act. If we talk about bank robbers, does it encourage our children to rob banks? If we talk about cleaning the house or the yard, do children want to run out and do it? If we talk excitedly about art, writing or football, does it mean that children will be interested in those activities? Talking about something does not necessarily increase the likelihood that it will occur.

---

[2]    *see Appendix 2, Page 157.

## OVERCOMING COMMON ROADBLOCKS

✓ Because of its intimate nature, talking about sex makes most of us nervous and embarrassed. Additionally, not having role models in our own parents leaves us unprepared to start the conversation with our children.

✓ Our self-made roadblocks increase as the child gets older. An initial conversation that is relatively easy with a 4 to 5 year old may feel more difficult with a 10 year old or a teenager.

✓ As parents, we may worry we will be asked a question that we can't answer or that we will look silly, nervous or awkward. It is perfectly acceptable to say to a child that we do not know the answer to a question, but that we will find out and talk more. There are reference books available in the library[3] and reliable information can be found on the Internet. Some school health teachers, nurses or doctors can also help answer questions.

✓ Some parents assume that independent, growing teenagers will do what they want regardless of any parental conversations. Parents may think that talking to teens won't make a difference. But in fact, <u>children look to their parents for guidance, even though they don't always say they do</u>. Most young people rely on parents to protect them. When adolescents are asked who are the most influential people regarding their sexual decisions, parents are at the top of the list.

✓ Parents may worry that a child will ask about a parent's own sexual behavior as a youth. Power Parents may or may not choose to share this information. It is always your choice. If possible, it is best to be direct and respond to questions about your feelings

---

[3]   See Appendix 1 P. 156

and experiences. If you are uncomfortable with sharing your own history, you can say, "I can understand that you may be curious about me and my behavior, but in many ways sex is personal. What is most important is helping you figure out what <u>you</u> believe and what <u>you</u> will decide to do about sexual activity."

## WHEN DO YOU START TALKING ABOUT SEX?

### POWER POINTS FOR POWER PARENTS:

- **ANY AGE IS A GOOD AGE TO START RAISING THE ISSUES OF SEXUALITY WITH CHILDREN, THE EARLIER THE BETTER.**

- **FIND OPPORTUNITIES IN DAILY LIVING AND THE MEDIA TO OPEN THE CONVERSATION.**

- **SPEND 15 MINUTES A DAY WITH YOUR CHILD EVERY DAY DISCUSSING A WIDE VARIETY OF ISSUES. A DISCUSSION OF SEXUALITY WILL THEN BE MORE NATURAL.**

- **FIND OUT WHAT IS BEING TAUGHT ABOUT SEX IN SCHOOL**

✓ At any age, some conversation about sex is better than none at all. It is best to begin when a child is young, and we need to respond when the child's questions first start. If children are curious enough to ask questions, they are old enough to receive simple, truthful and age-appropriate answers.

✓ An alert parent need not wait for questions. A person can make sex an acceptable topic to discuss by their openness. Look for "teachable moments" or "talk opportunities" which may begin when the child is even 4 or 5 years old.

Good openings/opportunities/events are:

- o Pregnancy in relatives, friends or neighbors
- o Observations of people's behavior, such as hand holding or kissing
- o Animal mating behavior or births
- o Television programs showing issues of relationships, puberty, dating, pregnancy, sexuality, fidelity and infidelity
- o Magazine articles and pictures that show our bodies
- o Planning for the onset of puberty

✓ For many younger children and preteens, discussing general issues from the news, television, and newspapers can be useful. When issues of sexuality and relationships become a usual topic that a parent discusses, more sensitive topics become natural and easier.

✓ Make it a point to spend 15 minutes a day with your child talking about whatever they want to discuss—what occurred at school; what is going on with their friends; what they saw on television; events in the family or in the village. When talking between parent and child is routine and expected, it is much easier to integrate issues of sexuality, love and relationships, as well as health issues such STI's and HIV as "Just something you and your child talk about."

✓ Sexual conversations are a process, not a one-time talk. You don't have to cover everything at once. In fact, it is often better to discuss these issues in bits and pieces, going only as far as the child is prepared to go. You can continue or add more later.

✓ Ask what is being taught in school about health, reproduction, illness, pregnancy, faithfulness, HIV and sexual protection. What texts or workbooks are being used? Suggest that you both look at the books. This is a wonderful way to utilize printed material as a foundation for a discussion. You can ask, "What do you think about this issue or this chapter? What did the teacher say? Did you understand this part? Tell me a little about what you understood. What do your friends say?"

Some parents may assume that if these issues are being taught at school, further conversation at home is not necessary. Don't be misled. School is an appropriate place for the "facts," the "mechanics" and the "biology" of sexuality. However, it is much more difficult for teachers to instill values, morals and beliefs, especially when there are 25 or more peers in the room. Schools may assign readings to students on sexuality issues, but often do not answer questions or clarify misconceptions.

✓ Even if these conversations have not been begun by parents early in a child's life, IT IS NEVER TOO LATE TO START! If you are reading this book, you are taking the first step. If your child is already a teenager, these conversations can still be immensely valuable.

✓ When sexual issues are being discussed for the first time, the biggest trap for parents is feeling that they need to "catch up" in one sitting. Doing this is ineffective and too much for the child. If your child is overwhelmed, further conversation may be more difficult.

## POWER POINTS FOR POWER PARENTS:

- **YOUR ATTITUDE IS MORE IMPORTANT THAN YOUR KNOWLEDGE**

- **LISTEN AND BE CURIOUS WITHOUT BEING INTRUSIVE**

- **SEPARATE FACT FROM OPINION**

- **GIVE AGE-APPROPRIATE ANSWERS TO ANY QUESTIONS ASKED**

✓ Your attitude and the way you talk are more important than what you say. Most importantly, you want to create a feeling that sex and sexuality are safe and acceptable topics.

✓ LISTENING is much more important than talking. Your tasks are to listen, learn, answer questions and provide clarification. You do not need to be a moruti. **Preaching does not work and does not help.**

✓ Conversations about sex involve fact, opinion and values. Facts are necessary, but opinions and values are crucial as well. If you are asked, your opinion should be given after you explore briefly why your child wants to know. This will provide the opportunity to learn about your children's concerns before influencing them with your thoughts. For example, if a teen says "What do you think about people having sex before they are married?" Initially a parent might say "We certainly can talk about that. What brought it to your mind?"

In response to your asking, sometimes your child will describe a thought, feeling, worry or situation that precipitated the question. Your response can be guided by what he or she says. Don't be surprised however, if the child says, "I was just wondering," and not go further. In any case, say what you believe in a few short sentences. Follow this up with, "So that's what I think. What do you think?"

✓ It is important that parents clearly separate their opinions and values from facts. If parental <u>opinions</u> are communicated as if they are <u>facts</u>, older children will quickly recognize this. For example, if it has been a mother's experience that men are untrustworthy, she may present this to her child as fact by saying: "Men are liars and can't be trusted to tell the truth or behave responsibly." This is <u>not</u> a universal fact. There are many good, honest and trustworthy men in Botswana, but it may have been this woman's experience to have been involved with dishonest and undependable men. If this is presented as a universal truth about all men however, the child will be confused. They will have already come into contact with some good men, and will not know how to deal with this new "fact" told by an influential parent. If it is repeated, this kind of interaction can color a child's attitude toward all men for a lifetime.

✓ Fit the Conversation to the Child's Age and Maturity

Whenever a parent talks with a child about sexuality and sexual behavior, it is important to know at what age sensitive topics can be understood. This allows you to answer questions with age-appropriate information given in ways helpful to the child. What follows is a list of children's ages and what most children of that age can understand. Each child matures at a different rate though, and girls often mature faster than boys. Therefore, no table of ages can be exact. Each parent must assess how these suggestions fit for their particular child.

## Sexual behavior at a young age

### Ages 3-4

◆ Children are curious about their bodies. This is a normal part of growing up. From the beginning, it is best to use correct terms such as penis, vagina and breasts. This is better than using nicknames, "silly" names or avoiding mentioning sexual organs altogether. It also sets the stage for later, more detailed conversations. In primary school, it may be helpful to talk with the teacher to find out what body parts are being discussed in school, and what names are being used. Consistency is useful.

◆ Also children at this age will touch their genitals—during a bath or when getting dressed. Children do so with no sense of modesty or shame. They are simply curious about a feel-good body part. It is important that toddlers should not be slapped, scolded or made to feel ashamed for being interested in their bodies. At this age, it is probably best just to ignore this touching behavior and distract the child with another activity.

◆ Children now can understand <u>where</u> a baby comes from, even if they don't understand the details. "All women have a uterus inside their body (the sack where the baby grows), and that's the place the baby stays until it is ready to be born."

### Ages 4 to 5:

◆ To the question of <u>how a baby is born</u>, a good answer at this age is—"When the time is right and the baby is big enough inside the uterus, the baby comes out through the Mommy's vagina, and is born." Perhaps at this age, the child may have seen a birth in animals and this similarity can be pointed out. If the child has never seen an animal birth, the parent might try to set this up with a neighbor who has a pregnant dog, cat or a farm animal at the lands.

## Conversation starters for younger children (4-5)

*Do you know the name for this? (pointing to a body part)*

*Your sister/aunt/friend's mother is pregnant. Do you know what that means? ("It means they are growing a baby inside of them")*

## Common Situations that Arise In 7-9 Year Olds

At this age, the question of <u>how</u> babies are made will come up and it is an age-appropriate question.

- ◆ "The Mommy and the Daddy love each other very much. They get close and touch each other. Then a Mommy's egg and a Daddy's sperm join and a baby begins to grow."

- ◆ It is also useful to begin to put sexual activity in its appropriate context of love and caring. "When people love each other, they want to show it. This is one of the ways that Mommies and Daddies are able to show this love."

- ◆ Eventually, a seven to nine-year-old will begin to ask, how does the sperm and the egg join? A simpler answer is better than a complicated one—"Daddy's and Mommy's need to be close enough so the sperm can come out of the Daddy's body and get to the Mommy's body.

- ◆ Many younger children ask the same questions over and over. Try to be consistent in your answers. This repetition helps the child learn and remember correctly. If a question has been asked and answered three or four times, a parent can also say, "I bet you know the answer to that one. We have talked about it before". If the child continues to "not know" the answer even though it has been repeated, provide the answer to them again and suggest that "Later I am going to ask you to see if you remember." If a child then gets it right, give positive praise.

♦ Also don't be surprised if children this age bring up topics of sex or sexuality at unexpected or awkward times or in situations that might be embarrassing. It could happen while waiting in the queue at the grocery or when you are eating a family meal. Children this age are naturally curious and old enough to begin formulating questions, but not old enough to always know the proper setting to ask.

♦ When this happens, you can give a partial simple explanation at the time or give a positive reaction without providing specific information. For example:

While standing in the checkout queue at Choppies, your 7 year old child exclaims, "Why is that lady so big?" while pointing to a pregnant woman. You respond "That's a good question. She is going to have a baby and we can talk about it when we are in the car."

✓ Most importantly, <u>don't ridicule and embarrass your child for asking a simple question</u>, with responses like "Shhh . . . don't say that and don't point." "Don't bother me." or "Not now Thabo, that's rude."

## A SAMPLE SITUATION FROM OUR STORY

One day, Kefentse and Bopelo were watching television, and the actors on the screen engaged in a long passionate kiss. Kefentse asked Bopelo what he thought about kissing.

"Oh come on Mama, you know I don't like anything about girls."

"So you and your friends never talk about kissing girls?"

"Once in a while we see the kids in Standard 7 fooling around and one time I saw them kiss, but you catch germs from doing that."

"It's normal for boys your age to not be interested in girls, but I think you'll find that that your feelings change when you get a little older. It will probably happen gradually, but you'll find that you want to be with girls and they want to be with you. It's fun to do things together."

"I don't know if that will happen—girls don't even like lizards and frogs and stuff."

"That's true now but some day you will want to be close to a special girl. You will want to hold her hand, touch her and have her touch you. It will feel good to both of you, but that is for a later time. From now on, I hope that we can continue to talk about boys and girls and their friendships. I will always be here to talk with you about anything. I can answer questions too. So can your father. Do you have any questions now?" (Pause) . . . Bopelo looked apprehensive. This was an invitation that he did not expect. Children were not supposed to ask questions. He didn't know if it was acceptable even though his Mama was asking. At times, some things had passed through his mind that he might want to know, but he always thought it was not right to ask. Today he felt close to his Mother and took a chance:

"Well . . . I was sort of wondering . . . how are babies made?"

"That's a really good question. When a Daddy and a Mommy love each other they want to show each other. There are the special parts of our bodies are just for showing that love and to make a baby. You know that boys have a penis and girls have a vagina—the parts of their bodies designed to make babies?"

"Yes, we learned that in science class."

"How about sperm and eggs?"

"The teacher told us that the man's sperm and the woman's egg get together to start the baby."

"That's right. Do you have any other questions right now?"

"Not right now."

"OK. I hope that you will come to me or your father with any questions about babies, being with girls or anything else that you want to ask about. That is part of my job as your mother to help you learn and to be ready to be a young man."

## Preteens—Ages 10 to 12

✓ By this age a child can handle a simple explanation of almost any topic involving sexual activity. The parent should answer any specific questions as they are asked or inquire about the child's understanding of things they may see in the media, in the neighborhood, or among their peers.

✓ Begin explaining the physical and emotional changes that happen during adolescence and puberty. Expect questions about topics that puzzle children or create strong feelings. These issues may be seen on TV, in magazines, in the movies, or have occurred at school or in friends' families. Children need to understand subjects that scare them, amuse them, puzzle them or create strong emotions. These can include issues about love, relationships, masturbation, homosexuality and pregnancy as well as dangerous activity such as sexual abuse and rape.

## A SAMPLE SITUATION FROM OUR STORY

When he was 12, Bopelo approached his Standard 4 teacher, Mr. Cheva, after school was done. Bopelo had an especially close relationship with this caring teacher.

"Mr. Cheva, do you know anything about how big a penis should be?'

"That's an interesting question. What makes you think of it?"

"When I was in the toilet yesterday, some of the Standard 7 boys were taking out their penises and talking about who had the biggest one. Then they started laughing at Penyo because they said he had a really small penis."

"Well, sometimes boys will do that. They think that having a big penis means that they will be big, strong men. They also think that if a boy has a smaller penis, he won't become a real man. Did they say something like that?"

"Yeah. The boy who had the biggest penis said that he was a 'bull' and that he could get any girl that he wanted. What did he mean? I don't get it."

"Some boys think that if they have a big penis, it is a sign of manhood and that girls will like them. So, just as a bull is big and strong, they think they will be, and that girls will like that too."

"Is that true?"

"No. The size of a boy's penis has nothing to do with his being a strong man.

The penis is just a special body part but its size does not say who will be a good man or a strong man. Girls will like boys who are good men, kind to them and respectful. The size of a penis has nothing to do with that. Boys sometimes don't know that. They do not yet know that being a real man means much more than having a penis.

## Conversation starters with 9-12 year olds

*How do you feel about becoming a teenager?*

*We all change a lot when we go through the teenage years. What have you heard or seen?*

*People can change when they become teens. Have you seen any changes in some of your friends yet? For example, sometimes boy's voices will sound different and girls start to grow breasts.*

*Are boys and girls treated differently in school? How? What do you think about that?*

*When do you think boys and girls should begin dating or "hanging out?"*

*Have any of your friends begun to have special" girlfriends" or "boyfriends?"*

Older pre-teens and teenagers spend a great deal of time wondering if they are "normal." It is very helpful, for children to understand that everyone is different and unique. Not being the same as everyone else is good and special. It is also at this age that friendships with both girl and boy friends take on a new intensity.

## A SAMPLE SITUATION FROM OUR STORY

Kagiso was 12 years old and Kefentse was now aware that crucial developmental issues would be arising as she was becoming a teen. One day, returning home from work, Kefentse found Kagiso in her room. Kagiso had obviously been crying.

"Kagiso, dear. What is wrong?"

"Nothing."

"But it looks like you've been crying and you seem upset."

"I was sort of messed up today, but I'm OK now."

Even as she spoke, tears began again and Kagiso turned away from her mother. Kefentse sat on the bed and put her arms around her daughter. She just held her, saying nothing. Kagiso began to sob and clung to her mother.

"It was so horrible. Lebogang came up to me when I was with Modise. She began telling him that I was cheating on him with Tuelo. She said that I had been sitting on Tuelo's lap at tea time and that we had been hugging. It is not true but Modise got mad at me and said he was no longer my boyfriend. I'm so mad at Lebogang and now I don't have a boyfriend either." Kagiso shook with emotion.

"Oh, I can see why you are so upset. Lebogang has been your best friend since Standard 4. And it sounds like Modise has become special to you too."

"I thought Lebogang was my friend but she's a liar and I hate her."

"I can see how you would feel that way. It makes me wonder why Lebogang would do that to you. Do you have any ideas?"

"I think she has been jealous of Modise and me. She said last week that we don't hang out together as much as we did. She doesn't have a boyfriend."

"Well, maybe Lebogang was missing you and your friendship. What she did was not right and I can see why you are hurt. What do you think would be the best thing to do now?"

"I don't know. Lebogang has texted me three times but I just won't answer. I texted Modise but he didn't answer. I don't know what to do to get him back."

"Well, maybe this will take time to sort out. For now, how about you come to the kitchen and have some tea with me. We can talk more if you like and maybe come up with a plan for school tomorrow."

"OK

## Ages 12 and older

✓ By this age, children are beginning to formulate their own values. More than ever, a parent needs to be in touch with a teen's development and morals.

✓ At the same time, a child will want privacy, so there must be a careful balance between inquiring, observing and allowing time for a child to be physically and psychologically more to himself or herself.

✓ Teens are beginning to establish their own peer group which will become much more important over the next several years. Peers will share deeply held confidences, worries, triumphs and secrets that will not be shared with parents. If a parent is too intrusive, the teenager will be less forthcoming and more likely to avoid the parent altogether.

✓ As teenagers, children begin to understand complicated relationship issues like separation, divorce, second spouses, step-parents, blended families and infidelity. When discussing these topics, it is important to try to be even-handed about issues and avoid being overly critical, demeaning or judgmental.

## CONVERSATION STARTERS FOR TEENS: COMMUNICATING VALUES

### POWER POINTS FOR POWER PARENTS:

- **YOU CANNOT INSIST THAT CHILDREN HOLD PARTICULAR VALUES, BUT YOU CAN HELP GUIDE THEM TO FORM THEIR OWN VALUES**

- **YOUR ACTIONS SPEAK LOUDER THAN YOUR WORDS**

✓ Children want and need moral guidance from parents. With this guidance children can learn to cope with their own emotional and sexual feelings, and with peer pressure. Talking about values helps develop guidelines for loving relationships, making it less likely that children will fall victims to emotional, physical or sexual abuse.

✓ Young people are actually <u>less</u> likely to engage in risky sexual behavior if they understand family values, have solid factual information and a connection to caring adults whom they can trust. Positive parent/child relationships also increase the child's self-esteem and confidence. These qualities lead to increased empowerment, solid decision-making skills and clarification of their own values.

✓ Sex and sexuality involve much more than just mechanics. Talking about romance, relationships with the opposite gender, love and commitment are all part of talking about sex. It is important that such discussions do not focus solely on the risks and dangers of sexual behavior such as STI's, HIV, and unwanted pregnancy. These interactions should also include the enjoyable and pleasurable parts of being a sexual individual. Other important pieces of the discussion are the joy of falling in love, the trust that develops between faithful partners, mutual respect, the benefits of partners growing old together and the increased self-esteem that comes with a healthy sexual relationship.

✓ As much as parents might sometimes wish to have it be so, it is very difficult if not impossible, to <u>make</u> a child have a certain opinion or value. It is much more successful, to help a child <u>clarify his/her own values</u>. Leading by example and inquiring about the child's thoughts and feelings result in a confident and self-assured teen. Preaching and lecturing do not work.

◆ For example, it is better

## To ask:

*"What do you think about a 15 year old becoming pregnant? Is she ready physically and emotionally? Would she miss out on things for herself if she has to leave school and raise an infant?"*

## Not Preaching:

*"Stay away from boys. If you fall pregnant, you will never have a life and your father and I will be very upset with you."*

No matter at what age a parent talks with his/her child about sensitive issues, keep it brief. Considering children's short attention spans, it is better to have three shorter conversations over several weeks or months than have one long talk. If there is something important left unsaid, it can always be added at a later time. Also, if the parent can return to an issue at a later time, it gives the child permission to do the same.

## Convenient phrases useful in these circumstances include:

*"I was thinking abut he conversation we had last week . . ."*

*"You said something interesting when we talked over the weekend . . ."*

*"I liked the talk that we had in the car. Did you have anything else to say about that?"*

*"I was hoping we could continue the talk we were having when we took the walk the other day . . ."*

*"I have been thinking since we had that discussion during school break how empowered you were to share your thoughts with me. I know it was a talk we might not have had in the past, but I hope you will continue to be that open with me. Has anything else been on your mind?"*

✓ Unless sexuality conversations have been common all along, be aware that the first time or two a parent talks about this with teens, they may be very cautious. They may even ask "Why are you talking about this?" You can truthfully answer: "It is part of my job as a parent to help you grow up safely, and learn how to make smart decisions. Talking helps us understand each other and stay in touch. It is important for both of us."

✓ At all ages, a person's actions and behaviors are much more significant than a person's words. This is especially true for a parent when a child begins to reach adolescence. Children will be watching what parents do and how they do it, while at the same time giving the impression that they don't care. Children model what they see. <u>A child will copy your actions, not your words.</u>

✓ As a Power Parent, do you have personal behaviors that you need to assess or change in order to be a positive role model to your kids?

For example—
*How do I treat my partner?*
*How do I disagree with my partner?*
*How much alcohol do I drink?*
*Do I drink responsibly?*
*Do I drink and drive?*
*What type of clothes do I wear?*
*Are they too tight?*
*Do they reveal too much of my body?*
*How do I behave around the opposite sex?*
*Am I respectful?*
*Do I avoid flirting or other inappropriate behavior?*

✓ Encourage your children to raise any fears or concerns that they have. While a parent may open a topic for conversation, it is useful to let children feel that they are in charge of an intimate discussion, not you. Let their questions and comments guide the conversation rather than trying to stick to a pre-planned agenda.

✓ <u>You may need to encourage them to be open with you more than once. Remember, this has not been the tradition in Botswana.</u>

✓ Children and teens **<u>must</u>** know that sensitive conversations with a parent will remain <u>private</u>. Of course, it may be useful and necessary to share the nature of these conversations with your spouse, but strictly avoid sharing confidential information with siblings, relatives, neighbors or friends. If a child learns that their "private" talk with you was revealed to another person, it will be the last time that your child takes the risk to trust you with sensitive information.

## UNDERSTANDING YOUR CHILD'S VALUES

✓ It is helpful to be curious about your child's thoughts without being intrusive, demanding or critical. Questions that invite children to talk with you include:

*What do you think about this?*
*How did you come to believe that?*
*What do your friends say about this?*
*Did you learn about this in school?*
*What was taught?*
*What reaction did you have to that lesson?*
*Help me understand why you feel that way . . .*
*What are the advantages and disadvantages of doing things that way?*
*What are <u>your</u> goals?*
*Would this behavior help to achieve those goals?*

✓ Help your child explain their thoughts and beliefs. Useful ways to encourage and elaborate conversation include:

*"Tell me more about that"*

*"Go on . . ."*
*"Can you say anything else about that?"*
*"That's interesting" (Then ask a clarifying question)"*

## WHEN YOU DON'T AGREE

✓ There will be times when our children express a belief or opinion that is different or even the opposite of what we, as parents, think is right or healthy. Sometimes, especially with teens, children will say something to their parents that is controversial or even outrageous. This can be a test to see how the parents are going to react. Teens may not fully believe what they are saying, but are waiting to see how the parents' response.

✓ If parents "fail" the test by immediately exploding, preaching, correcting or berating them, teens will learn that the parent is not really open to discuss sensitive topics or issues where the child feels differently than the parent. The child will hesitate to confide other genuine issues, now convinced that they will be met with a similar reaction.

✓ Expressing shock, disbelief or anger at what a teen says will seldom change the situation. Telling the child they "cannot" feel the way they do seldom makes them alter their opinion. (Did you initially accept your parent's ideas about all topics? Are there issues even now, where you don't see eye-to-eye with your parents?)

✓ When you disagree with your child's viewpoint and realize that you are too upset or angry to respond in a helpful way, take a "time out." Pause for a bit, go for a walk or just relax. You can always get back to your child with a calm response like:

*"That's an interesting way to look at it"* (It is not *"wrong"*, it is *"interesting."*)
*"I have to be honest, I see it this way . . ."*
*"Have you thought about the consequences of doing it that way?*
*"Here's another way to look at things . . ."*

✓ Don't insist that teens change their minds when a controversy or difference of opinion arises. A true Power Parent understands that the development of values is a process—a child needs time to think about what is right or wrong.

## WHERE TO TALK?

✓ Good conversation can take place anywhere, but <u>it is always</u> <u>best done in private</u>—sitting under a tree, on a walk, in the car, or at home.

Don't raise delicate issues at family gatherings, at dinner (unless it is just the two of you), when the children are with their friends or when siblings are within hearing.

## THE DO'S AND DON'TS OF CONVERSATIONS

### <u>Do</u>

Spend at least 15 minutes of "special time" with your child each day
Listen
Follow the child's lead on topics
Clarify issues that you do not understand
Stay informed about child development from reliable sources
Get "inside the shoes" of your children and try to look at things from their point of view
Remember how <u>you</u> felt as a child/teen

## Don't

Avoid or ignore your child, assuming they will turn out OK on their own

Preach

Crush a child's ideas or beliefs without an opportunity to talk

Feel like you are the only one with the right answer

Be overly critical

Yell

Embarrass your child

Threaten

## DEALING WITH TEENS

### POWER POINTS FOR POWER PARENTS:

- **PARENTING A TEENAGER CAN BE HARD. THE TEEN YEARS PRESENT A NEW PHASE THAT WILL CHALLENGE YOU**

- **"GOOD" KIDS CAN SHOW REBELLIOUS, PUZZLING OR ANGRY BEHAVIOR AS THEY BECOME TEENS**

✓ Even when you have had the opportunity to Power Parent early in a child's life, when children become teenagers, the developmental process changes and becomes more challenging. Teens develop new interests, new activities and begin to form their own social life. They become more independent in small and large ways, pushing themselves away from parents. This is a necessary stage for teens in order to mature and strengthen their own identity. You may observe that when the child was 11, he/she thought you were wonderful and wise. But that same child at 13 year may think you are inept, old-fashioned and a source of embarrassment.

✓ Teens start to confide more in their peers. They also want and need their own privacy. It is most important that as a parent, you not take these changes personally. They do not represent disagreement with your views or your beliefs, or a rejection of you as a parent. They are simply part of teenagers learning about who they are. Teens more than ever, need love, guidance and support of their parents. Parental guidance, though needed, must be carefully balanced to avoid becoming either over controlling or overly passive.

✓ While these complex behaviors between teens and parents are occurring, the teen's behavior may vary between being annoying, rude, irresponsible, rebellious, or even illegal. Just when a parent is wringing his/her hands in total frustration, the child can return to being the smart, cooperative person you remember. Fortunately, most kids who show temporary adolescent rebellion do not get into permanent or serious trouble. They grow up to become responsible and caring adults.

Despite irritating, provoking and even alarming behavior on the part of the child, parents need to show kindness and respectful communication. Firmness and authority will also be needed to set limits. <u>Consistent and positive parental attitudes and behaviors are the most powerful ways to communicate with and guide a teenager</u>. Even if it is not apparent, teens watch parents closely. They absorb and often repeat what they have experienced with their parents. Ironically, this may be at the same time that they are verbally saying that they wish to be "nothing like you."

## Conversation Starters with Teens:

*"How have you changed in the last several years?"*
*"What physical changes do you notice?"*
*"What emotional changes do you notice?"*

*"What do you like about these changes? What don't you like?"*

*"At what age do you think a person is ready to have a serious relationship with a boyfriend or girlfriend?"*

*"How do you decide whether a person is a good or bad influence on you?"*

*"At what age do you think a person is ready to have sex?"*

*"What do your friends say about this?"*

*"How should a person decide this?"*

*"At what age you think a person is ready to become a parent?"*

## A SAMPLE SITUATION FROM OUR STORY

Gofaone was Kefentse's favorite niece. She was the eldest daughter of Kefentse's oldest brother and was in her first year of study at Molepolole School of Education. Gofaone was stunningly attractive, smart and a wonderful girl. Gofaone was visiting her Auntie Kefentse in Gaborone. They were enjoying a sunny day, relaxing on the patio.

"So, Gofaone, howzit?"

"My studies are going well. I really love the idea of being a primary school teacher and this program has a reputation of producing the best prepared teachers for that grade level in Botswana. I'm really excited about that and think I'll have no trouble finding a position when I get my diploma."

"That's really exciting news. It sounds like you really chose the best school to study. Have you made many friends?"

"Yeah. There are some new girls that I've met. Most of them come from villages around Moleps and then I also have my best friend from Rakops who is in my class. We all get along great together."

"That sounds wonderful. Being away from home for the first time can be lonely and friends can make all the difference. You haven't mentioned any boys in your classes? Is there anyone special that you like?"

Gofaone blushed intensely "Oh Auntie, you know that is not a question to ask!"

"Well, I know it is a question that is not usually asked from an adult to a young lady like yourself. But, it is natural to have a special man in your life.

You are an attractive and fun girl. I would expect that there might be a lot of boys that would like you as their special girlfriend."

"Well actually, there is a boy in my English class, Mothusi. I'm not sure he even knows I exist . . . I've been watching him since our classes began. He seems really smart and he's so hot. He probably will never even notice me."

"I'm not sure that's true. I expect he has probably already noticed you, but he may be shy. Have any of your girlfriends given you advice? I know when I was your age, I depended a lot on my girlfriends to guide me."

"Yeah. My friend from Rakops thinks like you, that Mothusi really has noticed me and has talked about me to his friends. She found out from talking with Ernest, another student that Mothusi thinks I'm pretty."

"Now, that does not surprise me at all."

"I'm going to wait and see what happens. There is a special first year party coming up and maybe he will ask me if I want to go with him. Would it be OK if I let you know if he does?"

"I'd love to hear about it, Gofaone. And, you know, I'm always here too when relationships and friendships are important for you to discuss. You are such a special girl and you are growing to be a very special woman."

## Summary and the Way Forward

- ✓ Botswana is rapidly moving into a world of economic, prosperity and middle class values

- ✓ Behaviors must change along with incomes and possessions or the country will deteriorate

- ✓ We <u>must</u> change as a society. It is essential to the survival of Botswana

✓ HIV has been here for two decades now and remains a killer of our people

✓ Parents <u>must</u> talk with children even about subjects that have been sensitive and taboo in the past

✓ Sex is natural and deserves discussion

✓ Age-appropriate discussions about topics of love, male-female relationships, STI's and healthy decision making need to be the goal of every Power Parent

✓ **Students**—Read this book and discuss it with your parents

✓ **Parents**—Read this book and discuss with your children

✓ **Guardians, Grandparents, Aunts and Uncles**—Read this book. Often, as has been the cultural tradition in Botswana, you are in a position to begin these talks

✓ **Healthcare workers, Social Workers, Guidance Counselors and Teachers**—As much as we would hope that these discussions happen at home, the burden may fall to you. Read this book so as to be the most competent professionals you can be.

✓ Change can be challenging and anxiety provoking.

✓ <u>Courage is not acting without fear, it is acting in spite of fear.</u> It is acting because something else is more important than fear. In this case, it is the very survival of our country

✓ **Be strong and change!**

# CHAPTER 15

## GABORONE, BLOCK 7

*As Kefentse read* Power Parents, *so many things came to her mind—excitement mixed with determination, new ideas as well as some apprehension. She read quickly and with interest, often stopping to re-read passages that were especially important.*

*She turned the last page, sat thinking and knew the messages were right. She needed to change and she hoped she could do it, but it was scary. Talking about emotional parts of life was not part of her upbringing. Although she had been successful at most things, she worried that she might fail at the very things that were most important to her—being a successful parent to her three children. This book could be her roadmap. It laid out a plan that she could use for each of her children in simple, direct and practical ways. She needed to be a Power Parent and this book would be her guide.*

*She wanted to involve Tsiamo in this process. He had always been her partner, her rock and her strength. He was so smart, and such a good person. They would do this together.*

*That weekend, she found a quiet time to sit with him and begin talking about her ideas that she had found written in the Power Parents book. She talked about what she felt they needed to do. Tsiamo listened as he always did, but appeared concerned and puzzled.*

*"Kefentse, where are you getting these ideas? I was raised by my family without this sort of thing, and you were too. What makes you think it is so important? It makes me nervous to think about having to talk about something so delicate and private, like sex . . . and with children no less."*

Kefentse remembered many of the points that had been mentioned in the section on "Why these Conversations with Children are Important", and began to tell Tsiamo. She emphasized to him, that this was essential for their children's safety and happiness. "It's going to be new for me too, but we just *have* to do this." Tsiamo listened but seemed impatient, and it was clear that he was not totally accepting the idea.

"Don't you know how hard I'm working in Ramotswa? In addition to the long hours, I have a one hour commute each way. I'm exhausted when I come home, and it takes me most of the weekend to relax. I just feel stressed, and it's hard for me to think about taking on this kind of task with the kids when I already have so many things on my mind."

Kefentse knew that there was much truth in what he said. He often left the house at half six in the morning and would not return until almost seven. She was aware that he had begun to drink alcohol. Although he had never been much of a drinker, he now was drinking several beers almost every night. She began to worry about him. She knew that even when he was not drinking, he did not spend as much time with the children as she would have liked.

"What if Kagiso gets AIDS?" she pointed out. "These reasons you are giving for not being an involved, active parent will seem pretty small then."

Eventually, Tsiamo said he would think about it and let her know, but Kefentse had the feeling that he was just putting her off.

As always when she set her mind to something, Kefentse was determined to have the two of them change as parents. After a week, without further comment from Tsiamo, she again decided to bring up to him the need for conversation with the children. One evening, the children were playing with their cousins and the couple was relaxing on the patio. Before she could bring up Power Parents, Tsiamo said that he had something important that he wanted to discuss.

Tsiamo held Kefentse's hand and told her, "I have some really important news. I am being transferred to Ghanzi . . . It is an important promotion with a salary increase and there will be more advancement in the future. This is a really a big move up and one that could lay the groundwork for the rest of my career."

Kefentse was stunned. Didn't he realize that this meant he would be spending most of his days far from the family? Many thoughts quickly filled her mind. She had her job at the University, and it was unlikely that she could find a similar position in smaller, more rural Ghanzi. The kids were settled in their classes and would not want to start in new schools. Also they would be unhappy leaving their friends and family in Gaborone. The plan to raise the issue of parenting quickly fell out of the conversation. This transfer was going to overshadow everything.

Kefentse and Tsiamo talked more the next day about the job change. Both of them ultimately agreed that the best choice for everyone was for the children and her to stay in Gaborone while Tsiamo went to Ghanzi. He would return for visits whenever he could. He kept telling her "It will only be for a couple of years. The next promotion will be to the Ministry in Gabs, and I will be back."

Over the next month, plans were made and Tsiamo left for Ghanzi. Neither of them knew then how this development would forever change their lives.

# CHAPTER 16

## GHANZI, 8AM

Tsiamo awoke bleary-eyed. *His head was pounding and he felt sick at his stomach. He was naked, with his business suit, shirt and tie lying in a pile on the floor. He could hear the rattling of dishes from the kitchen, and his head began to clear. SHE was still here—the cute young junior manager from Maun . . . or was she from Kang? He was pretty sure that her name was Angelina, although he was not certain. He slipped into his bathrobe and headed to the bathroom. After splashing water on his face, he looked at his reflection in the mirror and wondered, "What have I done?" He walked hesitantly to the kitchen where a pretty girl offered him a cup of tea.*

*She looked at him and coyly said, "I've got to tell you something. You were pretty hot in bed last night. I didn't know that they made conference organizers so handsome and sexy."*

*For Tsiamo, events from the previous night gradually became clearer. It had been the third and last night of the annual Department of Transportation Workshop which his group in Ghanzi was hosting. Angelina was one of the conference attendees and seemed to be flirting with him from the very first day. At first it was just idle chatter during the conference breaks. Then the previous night, they decided to get a few drinks at the hotel bar, which turned out to be many more than a few.*

*Some of the details were still hazy, but he must have invited her back to his apartment. They had sex—he remembered that. He realized now that he did not know her at all—especially anything about her health history or HIV status. He was almost sure that she had not asked about this either. They had started to be physically affectionate at the bar then became urgently passionate as they came through his front door. No information, no condom, no protection. All he knew was that he was now in his kitchen with a stranger with whom he had just had risky sex. He had never before been unfaithful in his marriage and he wasn't totally sure why it happened now. But whatever the reasons, he just wanted to get this woman out of his home as quickly as possible. He didn't want to face her any longer and more importantly, face his own guilt.*

*After picking at some food, he made an excuse that he needed to go back to the conference venue. She said that was not a problem, because she had to return to Maun anyway. She made sure he had her phone number and invited him to call "any time" so that they could get together again and go to a "really fancy restaurant." It was not anything that she said directly, but Tsiamo distinctly felt that she was less interested in him and more interested in being involved with a well-paid manager who could take her to nice places. Sex without love had been empty. She did not know nor care about him. This only intensified his anger at her and himself.*

*There were no conference obligations for Tsiamo that morning. He just wanted to be out of the apartment and away from her. With tea and some food, he felt a little better. Driving out to a spot by the river, he sat in his car . . . just thinking. He was embarrassed, angry, guilt ridden and scared both for his own health and for his relationship with Kefentse. He had been unfaithful.*

*If Kefentse learned of this, how would she react? Was he infected with the AIDS virus? If he was, what would that mean? If he didn't know his status, would he be able to have sex with Kefentse without telling her? No, he knew he couldn't do that. If he was infected and gave her the virus, he couldn't live with himself. But he had to stop having sex with her, at least for a while, until he could be tested. He would have to think of some reason why they could not be physically together.*

*He wondered, "Should I tell her about being unfaithful and take the consequences?" He was afraid she might not forgive him. But would he have to tell her? Maybe he could just make up a story to avoid going home. Maybe his car would "break down" and not be drivable for weeks. Perhaps an "urgent assignment" would develop so that he could not leave Ghanzi for a while. If he managed to delay having sex for three months, he could take the HIV test. If it was negative, he might not have to tell her about the affair at all.*

*Part of him knew that he would feel less burdened if he got this off his chest and told her. Dealing with the guilt was already eating at him. But what would she do if she knew? Tsiamo know that Kefentse loved him very much but she was a determined woman. He also knew that breaking this news would be devastating for her. It all seemed so complicated. What _had_ he been thinking?*

*He began to make justifications to himself. He had been in Ghanzi for eight months now, seeing his wife and family only infrequently. A man like him had normal sexual urges. He knew he didn't want to use a prostitute—that would be really risky. But being abstinent on his part had become harder and harder. He felt that he had been deprived of the love and warmth of his wife and was forced to live far from his home. For a while, he was able to convince himself that he was "owed" a good time once in a while. Even if that were true—which somehow in his heart he knew it was not—why had he been so careless? He was smarter than that. AIDS warning messages were plastered all over Gaborone, Ghanzi and every other village in Botswana. He knew that a condom was the only way to have protected sex. Once he had actually meant to buy some condoms "just in case" but had never gotten around to doing it.*

*Finally he also had to admit to himself that during this time away, he'd begun to drink more heavily. What else was there to do? Watch television, read, and work. He had made a few male friends and they played pool and watched football matches. Even these activities had become boring unless he had a few beers. He didn't feel good about the alcohol, but at least it eased the loneliness. He was lost, confused and scared. After sitting for over an hour, he eventually returned to his apartment. He had made no decisions. Calling Kefentse and the kids that afternoon as he usually did, he attempted to sound upbeat and normal.*

*At work on Monday, Tsiamo tried to concentrate on his paperwork and meetings, but found himself more and more preoccupied with the feeling that he had been very, very wrong. He had violated his own principles, God's principles, and those of his family. The more he tried to bury the feelings, the more they kept bubbling up. As the week progressed, even three or four beers at night only dulled the guilt for a few hours, and every morning the sadness and anxiety reappeared.*

*Tsiamo went on this way for three weeks, feeling worse by the day. The time came for his regularly scheduled trip to Gaborone to see the family. He knew he had to make a decision. It became clear to him that he would never be able to keep this secret from Kefentse. He had to step up, be a man, admit his wrongdoing, and apologize. He would have to take the consequences. It was the only way he could live with himself.*

*Tsiamo arrived at home late on Friday from the long trip. He tried to make small talk, but felt he was carrying a 1000 kg weight on his shoulders. Both he and Kefentse were tired. The timing was not good, but he had to confess—the sooner the better. He told Kefentse they needed to talk after the children were in bed. He downed his third beer of the evening, sat on the patio and waited for her. When his wife sat down, it just started spilling out.*

*"I've got something to tell you, and it's not going to be easy. I don't know how you will react, but to be honest, this has been the most difficult three weeks of my life. I know myself enough to know that if I don't get this out, it is going to permanently scar me and our relationship. Three weeks ago, I slept with another woman. It was someone at the conference and it was only one time. I don't love her. It was after a night of heavy drinking, but I know that is no excuse. I was stupid and didn't use a condom. I have felt guilty and worried to the point that I have been having trouble working. I still don't know if I have caught any disease, and I can't be totally sure she's not pregnant. At least for now, you and I can't have any sex. It may sound silly after what I have done, but I care too much about you to take the risk that I might infect you."*

*(pause) "I can't really expect you to forgive me, because I haven't yet forgiven myself. I don't have anything else to say. I've told you what happened and that's all there is."*

*Kefentse sat frozen as tears began to roll down her face. She must be having a bad dream. It couldn't be that the man she cared about most, the one who* had shared her bed for the past 10 years, the one she had trusted and to whom she had given her heart had betrayed her. It was as if someone had thrown a spear into her soul; nothing could have hurt her more. She suddenly was confronted with a fear that she had had since Tsiamo's transfer to Ghanzi—a fear of losing him and the family life she loved.

In the determined manner that was her personality, Kefentse's sadness rapidly turned to rage. "You bastard! How could you do this to me and to our family? Right now, I hate you with every bone in my body. It's a small consolation that you don't want me to get an STI. But I guess I should be thankful for anything that comes from a person who is a cheat. No, I won't forgive you. Get out. I want you out of our bedroom and out of our home."

In a flash, the perfect world that Kefentse and Tsiamo had created, was shattered. Even while Tsiamo was reeling from the force of Kefentse's anger, he became panicked at the thought of losing everyone he loved.

For Kefentse, the rage masked the incredible hurt and despair that she felt. Once again, a man she loved had betrayed her. First it was Gape and now Tsiamo. Her broken heart could see no hope. She insisted that Tsiamo leave the house that evening.

He found a hotel room and began driving back to Ghanzi in the morning. His thoughts tumbled over and over. He couldn't have been more miserable. He had ruined his life and that of his family. By the time he reached his apartment, he was determined to do whatever it took to get his family back—but not now. Some time, space and healing was needed.

Kefentse had taken two sick days to recover from the acute shock of Tsiamo's confession, but even as she returned to work, she was simply going through the motions of her job. As several weeks passed, she gradually came to the realization that she must get on with her life. As some of her emotional strength returned, she was able to give more to the children. She didn't know if the relationship between Tsiamo and herself could be healed. What she did know was that she had to continue to give the children love, understanding and good parenting—even if she did it alone. She would be strong for her children and she would keep them safe.

Kefentse finished re-reading the section on "When Do You Start Talking about Sex." She knew that Kagiso was at the sensitive age where serious issues about relationships, sex and health needed to be discussed. But it might not be easy. Kagiso was exhibiting the expected turbulence of the teen years. She was moody, irritable and distant. This was especially so since Tsiamo had been transferred. For now, Kefentse thought, it would be more comfortable starting conversations with the other children.

Bopelo was only ten years old and still enjoyed being with his mother. Kefentse began taking time to spend 15 minutes a day just with him. This was their special time and turned out to be an unexpected pleasure for both of them. Kefentse decided to spend this quality time with Bopelo dealing with less sensitive subjects first, before addressing the issues of sexuality. Sometimes they played a game, sometimes they looked at his homework and other times, they watched television together. They talked easily about a variety of issues especially ones that interested him. Bopelo was a curious child, who often asked questions about all sorts of things. He seemed to readily accept his mother's replies. They established a routine of spending time together.

Ntume was a beautiful and inquisitive child. Even at her young age, she was always asking questions. Kefentse would pretend to be annoyed with all her chatter. In reality, she was pleased that young Ntume was so bright, curious and open. These qualities would be an important part of a healthy development.

One day, upon seeing her brother Bopelo using the toilet, Ntume approached her mother asking why Bopelo "had a stick to pee" and she did not?

*Kefentse recognized this as the first of many sexually related questions that Ntume would ask. She took the opportunity as a Power Parent to respond to Ntume's natural curiosity.*

*"What Bopelo has is called a penis. Every man has one . . . even your father. A penis is a boy's way of peeing. It is special to them and makes them different from girls."*

*"I want one of those."*

*"Well, girls have something different but it is special too. Girls have a tube inside that sends the pee from their bodies. It has a word that is a big name. It is called a urethra."*

*"That is a big name. U-ree-rah."*

*"U-wreath-rah. That will get easier to say when you are older."*

*"Can I see mine?"*

*"Not really. It is in your private parts down below in your panties."*

*Ntume pulled at her underpants, felt and tried to look. "I can't see it."*

*"That's OK. It is there. As girls, it is our way of peeing."*

*Several weeks later, Ntume came to Kefentse.*

*"Mommy, I just saw Mpho and her belly is so big! Has she eaten too much paleche?*

*"No, Ntume. Mpho is going to have a baby and the baby has been growing inside of her. So the big bump you see is the baby inside. The baby will be born very soon."*

*"How does the baby get out?"*

*"You remember us talking about girls having a urethra . . . the tube where pee comes out?"*

*"Yes. We have that tube and boys have a penis."*

*"That's right. All girls also have another special place in our private parts called a vagina. It is larger tube and when the baby is ready to be born, it comes out of this tube."*

*"Oh, so girls have two tubes . . . a small one for pee and a bigger one for a baby?"*

*"That's right"*

*"Well, I hope that the baby comes soon so we can play."*

# CHAPTER 17

## GABORONE, BLOCK 7

*WHILE THESE INTERACTIONS were occurring with the children, Tsiamo had started to call again. First, it was just to talk with the kids, which Kefentse knew she could not deny him. Although initially reluctant, Kefentse eventually had some conversations with Tsiamo even though at first, they were curt and short. Tsiamo pleaded for a second chance to come home and be a family again. Kefentse wasn't ready for that.*

## GHANZI

*Tsiamo was missing his family and very upset with himself. He had been thinking a lot about what he had done and about Kefentse's reaction. He desperately wanted to regain her trust. More than ever, he realized his terrible mistake, and wanted to be a better husband and father. What could he do? Suddenly it came to him—before his transfer to Ghanzi, Kefentse had asked him to read a book. What was the title? "Being a Better Parent"? "Parents Helping Kids"? . . . no it was "Power Parents." That was it. He went to Francistown for a meeting that week, bought the book, and began to read.*

*From the first page, the book was revealing to him. In it were ideas that were new and unfamiliar. It suggested that today's parents needed to behave differently than the parents of previous generations. He always felt he was a good father, but realized he had never really thought about what that meant. He had just assumed that he would raise his children as his parents had raised him. His mother had been the person who did most of the parenting especially when he was young. In his own family, Kefentse had followed that same pattern up to now. In thinking about it however, Tsiamo realized that neither his mother nor father talked with him about some very important issues, like sexuality. He remembered his parents mostly scolding him when he did wrong and telling him he should obey. As he reflected on the suggestions in the book, he realized that perhaps he had a lot to learn.*

*When Tsiamo read the part about the importance of spending time alone with his children, he knew that he had not been doing this very well for a long time, even before he had come to Ghanzi. He also knew that this was exactly what Kefentse had wanted. He decided that he would have Bopelo come to visit and the two of them could spend time as father and son. Focusing on what Bopelo needed would also keep Tsiamo from dwelling on the news he had just received.*

# CHAPTER 18

## GABORONE, BLOCK 7

*Bopelo was in the sitting room one evening as Kefentse was reading. She noticed that he had been in a chair, staring into space. This was unusual for him.*

*"Hey Bopelo, what is going on?"*

*"I have been thinking about Daddy. He has been gone a long time. He doesn't seem to call us much. Why?"*

*"Yes it has been a long time. He and I are spending some time apart right now because we're having some problems."*

*"What kind of problems?"*

*"They are big people problems for Daddy and me, and they do not have anything to do with you or your sisters. It's like when you and some of your friends have problems. Do you remember when Thato took your football and you were so angry? I know he gave it back, but for a long while you were very mad and did not want to be around him. It took a while for the two of you to be friends again. Your Daddy and I are having some disagreement about how we get along with each other and there are some angry feelings. It is very important though to remember that he loves you and your sisters very much. He wants to see you, but for now, he is staying in his apartment in Ghanzi until we get things worked out. What do you think about that?"*

*Based on his recent conversations with his mother, Bopelo was beginning to think that she really did want to know what was on his mind, so he had more confidence.*

*"Will he ever be coming back to stay with us?"*

*"I am sure he wants to stay with us. That has not changed. I hope things between us will be worked out soon. We have started to talk on the phone and make things better. He wants you to come and visit him next weekend."*

*Bopelo was thrilled.*

*Kefentse had found it hard to talk with Bopelo about the separation but she was trying. The situation with Kagiso was not going nearly as well. Since she had turned 15, there had been a marked change in Kagiso's attitude and behavior. She was spending more time in her room, wanting to be less with the family and more with her peers. Whereas Kagiso had been fun and easy-going for most of her earlier life, she was now quiet, moody, and tense around the family. There was little enjoyment in talking together or even being in the same room.*

*Kefentse noticed that since Tsiamo had been spending all his time in Ghanzi, Kagiso seemed even more distant and quiet. Any time that Kefentse started the simplest conversation such as," How was school today?" or "What are you doing this weekend?" Kagiso would grunt, shrug her shoulders or have an insulting remark.*

*Kefentse knew from reading "Power Parents" that emotions changed in adolescence, so she was not terribly surprised by this new behavior. She also wondered if the marital separation was affecting Kagiso's behavior. She was so quiet and distant that Kefentse did not know what was happening in her teen life. Most of all, Kefentse worried because she did not want Kagiso to make the same mistakes that she had made with Gape. Kagiso was 15 years old and had started her menstrual period two years ago. Although physically able to become pregnant, Kagiso was not nearly emotionally mature enough to become a parent. Kefentse worried that she and Kagiso were growing apart at a very vulnerable time. She was feeling disconnected from her daughter when she knew that her daughter needed her the most.*

*One evening when they were alone together, Kefentse took the opportunity to speak to Kagiso.*

"You haven't said much about it, but I was wondering what you think about your father being away for so long?"

Kagiso responded sharply.

"I don't like it. The last time he called, I asked him when he was coming back. He said that you were the one who sent him away and you didn't want him to come back."

"It is true that I was the one who asked for us to live separately for a while. Did he say anything else about why I did that?"

"No"

"The next time you talk to Daddy, ask him what happened. If he doesn't want to talk about it, ask him if you and I can discuss it.

After Tsiamo's next phone call, Kagiso said "Daddy didn't want to talk about any details of why he is not with us. He said that I should ask you."

"OK. You are old enough to hear about what happened and why I did what I did. While he was at work in Ghanzi, your Daddy had a sexual relationship with another woman. It hurt me very much because I felt it was terribly selfish on his part. He was not thinking about what was best for our family. I think faithfulness is very important and this was a big mistake. Because of this, I told him that I didn't want him to live at home. He and I have been talking on the phone and hope to work out our relationship. I think we are making some progress, but it has not been easy for me to trust him again. I want him to come home and be with us, but I have to know he is sure that the only relationship he wants is with me and no other woman. I also want him to be more involved with the three of you. I want him to spend time with you just having fun, helping with your homework or talking to you about important things. For example Kagiso, you are getting to the point where you may be interested in boys more than you have been up to this time. I think it's important for you to get a Daddy's view about this."

Kagiso did not respond to the explanation and after several minutes, she went to her room.

∽∾

*That weekend while Bopelo was visiting Tsiamo in Ghanzi, Kefentse and Kagiso were walking to the shops. Kefentse thought it a good time for a follow up conversation. She asked Kagiso if she had had any thoughts or feelings about their previous conversation.*

*Kagiso was quiet initially, but finally said, "I don't know what to think. Maybe it's true what they say that all men are just snakes and can't be trusted."*

*"I don't think all men are snakes and I don't think your Daddy is a bad man, even though what he did hurt me and our family very much."*

*(Pause)*

*"Have you ever slept with another man since you were married?"*

*Kefentse thought for a moment. In times past, she might have been upset that her daughter was so bold to ask such a private question. But a lot had changed in Botswana society and in Kefentse's own thinking. The Power Parents book had taught her the positive impact of openness and honesty*

*"No, I haven't. I can't say that I have never thought about it or been attracted to other men. But I have been faithful. Over the years, I found advice and strength in talking to my friends and in my spiritual beliefs. If I value and expect faithfulness from my husband, I have to honor the same rules.*

# CHAPTER 19

## GABORONE, BLOCK 7

*ONE EVENING, A soapie on TV showed a teenage girl just learning that she had fallen pregnant. But this girl didn't want to be a mother. Kefentse and Kagiso watched the story closely. The girl on TV decided not to tell her parents that she was pregnant. Instead, she was arranging for an abortion.*

*Kefentse took the opportunity to say to Kagiso, "Wow that is quite a situation for her."*

*"She was stupid to get pregnant."*

*"Why do you think she was stupid?"*

*(No response)*

*Kefentse: "I agree that it is not a good idea at her young age to have fallen pregnant, but it can happen sometimes."*

*More silence.*

*"Maybe we won't discuss this anymore right now, but I hope we can continue the conversation when you feel more like talking. I think the issue of relationships between girls and boys is important. It is something mothers and daughters should discuss."*

*Three days later, Kefentse and Kagiso were alone after dinner was finished. The other two children were playing in the living room. Kefentse said "You remember when we were watching that soapie a couple of days ago? I was hoping that we could talk some more about that girl becoming pregnant and her plan to have an abortion. I really am interested in what you think about this."*

*"I don't feel like talking about it with you. I just want to go out and be with my friends."*

*"I know you do and that's very normal for teenagers, but that doesn't mean that the two of us can't talk together about important things. You are quickly becoming a young woman. You are going to be faced with lots of challenges in the next few years like that girl on TV. One really serious thing in that program besides being pregnant was the issue of having an abortion. We both know that abortion is not legal in Botswana. Right?"*

*Kagiso nodded.*

*"Girls who have an abortion may be putting their life in danger. Do you remember last year the Form 4 girl who tried to end her pregnancy by seeing the street abortionist? She died from the potion that he gave her."*

*Kagiso gave no response.*

*"I just want to make sure that you know that I am here to talk about all these important decisions in your life and to support you. Dealing with dating, relationships, sex, falling pregnant, HIV, STI's, drugs and alcohol are all parts of being a teen in Botswana today. There are also going to be many pressures from your peers. I want you to be confident in what you believe."*

*(Pause)*

*Kagiso finally said: "I said that girl was stupid for falling pregnant. Do you think I'd be stupid like her?"*

*"No that's not what I'm saying. I simply want to find out what you are thinking. Having a baby is a life changing event for a woman at any age."*

*"Yeah, the friends of that TV girl told her not to hang out with that boyfriend. He was bad for her and could get her in trouble, but she didn't listen."*

*"Why do you think she didn't listen to her girlfriends?"*

*"I guess she thought she was in love."*

*"I think you're right. That girl really got blinded by love. It can be a pretty powerful emotion."*

*"I wouldn't know." murmured Kagiso.*

*"You may not have experienced that powerful love feeling yet, but you will. You're a pretty girl who is getting prettier and more attractive by the day.*

*Boys will see that too and want to be with you. Some day you're going to find yourself feeling very attracted to a boy. It is a very strong feeling. If it is real, true love, it will last and a deep relationship will develop between the two of you. It would not surprise me if you felt some of those feelings for someone during your teen years—many girls do. It can be easy to fall in love. But it takes time and getting to know someone to really find out if this is the right relationship for you."*

*Kagiso looked thoughtful as she got up to clear the dishes.*

# CHAPTER 20

## GABORONE, BLOCK 7

*KEFENTSE RE-READ THE Power Parents section on Listening to Children and was trying to practice with Kagiso whenever she could, but it was difficult. With few exceptions, Kagiso remained very difficult to approach.*

*One day, Kefentse received a call from Mma Gabathusi, the Guidance Teacher at Kagiso's school. She said that Kagiso's grades had dropped, she had been dodging classes and the day before, she got into a physical fight with another girl. Mma Gabathusi was concerned. "This is very unusual for Kagiso. She has been one of our better students and is a Peer Educator. Is there anything that could be upsetting her at home?"*

*Kefentse decided that she must tell Mma about the separation from Tsiamo. Mma Gabathusi reassured Kefentse that similar family situations occurred among students regularly. She wondered if Kagiso might be angry with her parents and this anger was now resulting in poor grades, truancy and fighting. Mma Gabathusi and Kefentse decided to meet together with Kagiso the next day.*

*As the meeting started, Kagiso came into the room and was surprised to see her mother. She quickly hid that response with downcast eyes.*

*Mma Gabathusi began the conversation: "We asked you here this afternoon Kagiso because your mother and I are worried about you."*

*Kagiso said nothing.*

*Kefentse spoke up. "Mma and I were wondering if you might be angry about something."*

*Kagiso remained silent.*

Kefentse continued. "I told Mma Gabathusi that your Daddy has not been living at home. I know this has this been upsetting you. Do you think there is a connection between this and what is happening here at school?"

Kagiso lashed out at Kefentse. "It's all your fault. I don't have a Daddy at home now just because you can't forgive him. Lots of other kid's fathers have girlfriends. I don't see why he can't come home."

"We will talk more about this at home and I can understand that you are upset. But your behavior at school must change. You are not allowed to dodge class, not finish your work or fight with other students. You will not be allowed to go out with your friends until we see an improvement here in school. Mma Gabathusi and I will be in touch with each other about your school performance."

# CHAPTER 21

## GABORONE, BLOCK 7

*Bopelo got off the bus from Ghanzi, ran happily to his Mother and spoke rapidly. "Mama, I had the best time! Daddy and I took these walks all around Ghanzi. We kicked the football and had fun. We talked about the Zebras team and all sorts of stuff. I did one of my drawings for him and he put it on his refrigerator. He even asked about what was going on in school. When can I go see him again?*

*"Maybe soon. We will see."*

*Kefentse was pleasantly surprised at Bopelo's description of the visit with his father. Tsiamo had never before spent such quality time with any of the children. Kefentse's mind started to churn.*

*Over the next week, she did a lot of soul-searching. It was going to take a leap of faith to trust Tsiamo. She was scared to let herself open up again to him. But Bopelo's account of how Tsiamo was more involved as a father, the positive telephone calls they had been having and her need for help with Kagiso's problem behaviors convinced her that it might be time for the two of them to get back together.*

*She called Tsiamo and told him that if he was ready, she was willing to have him return to the house on a trial basis. Tsiamo said, "I want this very much and now is a good time. There is a big transportation project in Gaborone starting next week. I can ask to be re-assigned. But before I come back, there is something else I need to tell you . . .*

# Chapter 22

## GABORONE, BLOCK 7

LESS THAN A *month after the first call from school and two weeks after Tsiamo returned home, Kefentse received another call from Mma Gabathusi. Mma said that Kagiso had again started to dodge classes and now was missing some school days altogether. It was very clear to Kefentse that just having Tsiamo at home had not been the solution to Kagiso's misbehavior.*

*That evening, Kefentse and Tsiamo talked about how to handle this increasingly serious problem. They decided that presenting as a united team to Kagiso was best. That evening they talked with Kagiso together.*

*Her mother began: "Kagiso, I received a call from Mma Gabathusi today saying that you have started to dodge classes again and sometimes you have missed the entire day."*

*"That's not true. She must be thinking of someone else.'*

*"Let us see your notebooks for the last month."*

*"I loaned some of them to Thato. She needed to copy some assignments."*

*"Let us see the ones you have."*

*Grudgingly, Kagiso got some notebooks from her school bag. There were many days of class notes missing from her books.*

*"Kagiso, we are upset that you have been missing classes at school, but we are more upset about your lying to your Daddy and me. Why are you doing that?"*

*"I don't know."*

*Tsiamo added, "You don't know why you are missing school or why you are lying to us?"*

*Kagiso raised her voice "School is dumb. I hate it."*

Kefentse responded, "And lying to us?"

"You just don't understand me."

Tsiamo said firmly, "We understand Kagiso, that you are a girl growing up. We understand that this can be very hard time. But as your Daddy I know that we not only love you, but we must help you through this time by keeping you safe and focused."

With tears starting, Kagiso said: "I don't need your help."

"Your Daddy and I think you do. So, you are not to go anywhere but to school and home until your school behavior and class work improve. In that time we hope you will help us understand what is going on with you. I will be in contact with Mma Gabathusi every day to make certain you are attending classes. Any further reports of problems at school or anywhere else, will be met with further restrictions and punishment. Do you understand?"

Kagiso nodded.

Tsiamo said gently: "We love you very much and will be here to talk with you when you are ready."

~~

Time seemed to pass uneventfully, but Kagiso remained distant and quiet. Tsiamo was showing much more interest in the children, and spending some special time with them each day. Ntume and Bopelo seemed to genuinely enjoy the time; Kagiso complied without much enthusiasm. Kefentse was delighted to see that Tsiamo's promise to change was turning into positive action.

Without her parents or Mma Gabathusi knowing, Kagiso was missing afternoon school activities. She had begun going to a bar where she met a man much older than herself.

By chance on her way home from work, Kefentse saw Kagiso walking away from a bar with an adult man. That evening, she talked with Tsiamo about what she has seen.

Kefentse began, "As I passed through the village today, I saw Kagiso coming out of Amo's bar. She was with a man whom I have seen before somewhere, but

I do not know him. The two of them were laughing and weaving unsteadily through the street until they disappeared around a corner. When Kagiso came home an hour later, I asked her what she had been doing. She said that she just 'needed to get out of the house' and was 'taking a walk by herself.' When I asked her, she said she hadn't been drinking."

Tsiamo was upset. "What is happening with our daughter? Kagiso has always been such a good girl."

"I don't know and I'm very worried. We now are sure she is still leaving school, drinking alcohol and seeing an older man. Both of us know he can have no good intentions in being with a girl as young as Kagiso. I am worried she may be taking whatever he offers and having sex with him."

Tsiamo thought for a minute. "I think you would agree that I have been more actively involved with the kids since I have been home, but I think this is a time as a mother for you to talk with Kagiso alone. This is a very sensitive area and Kagiso might be overwhelmed with both of us talking with her together."

Kefentse agreed but wasn't quite sure how she was going to handle the situation. They thought that first it would help everyone to get a night's rest. Kefentse would talk with Kagiso in the morning. Afterwards, she and Tsiamo would decide the way forward.

Early the next morning just after she awakened and before seeing Kagiso, Kefentse got a phone call from her sister Refilwe. Refilwe said, "Kagiso came to me yesterday concerned about having an infection 'down there.' She wanted me to take her to the clinic, but not tell you or Tsiamo. I was going to keep this between Kagiso and myself, but when I heard the results of the clinic visit yesterday, I decided that you and Tsiamo really needed to know. Kagiso was diagnosed with gonorrhea. You know that's a sexually transmitted illness. She has begun treatment which she has to continue for several weeks. The nurse said her pregnancy test was negative."

Kefentse was in shock. "Oh no! Do you know if an HIV test was done?"

"She was too young to have it done without your permission."

Thanking Refilwe and getting off the phone, Kefentse went to Kagiso's room. She told Kagiso that her Aunt had called.

Kagiso was angry. "She wasn't supposed to tell."

"I am glad she did," Kefentse responded angrily. "Tell me what is going on, <u>right now</u>."

All at once, Kagiso looked panicked and like a small girl, began crying.

"I started going to Amo's bar a few months ago with Koketso and Lebo. That's when we would leave school and dodge classes. I met this man who works in the furniture store. He said that I was pretty and that the next time I should come back by myself. I started to go see him almost every day. He was funny and good looking. He started giving me little gifts and said we could just 'hang out.' He would tell me how nice my hair was, what a nice body I had and how sexy I was. One time we walked down to a jewelry store and saw these sparkling green earrings. He said they would look great on me and make me look like a real woman, but that they were very expensive.

He bought me alcohol each time I was with him and about a month ago, he said that we should go to his car to have some private time together. He wanted to show me something. So I did. He pulled out this box and in it were the green earrings. He told me to try them on right there. Then he began to touch and kiss me telling me he loved me. He said that a woman who would wear those earrings was the kind of woman he wanted to be with. I began to feel scared, but sort of excited too. He said we should have sex to make us closer as a real couple. I said OK because I guess I thought I loved him too. I asked him if he had a condom. He said he was healthy and if I really loved him, I would trust him and we wouldn't need a condom. So I had sex without one."

Kefentse looked defeated. "What made you think he loved you?

"He said his wife no longer wanted to have sex with him, that she was old and tired. He said I was beautiful and sexy and that he wanted me. He said he <u>really</u> loved me."

At that point, Kagiso cried harder and could barely get the words out between her sobs.

"And then I get this awful stuff leaking into my underpants. It smelled and I was so scared. That's when I talked with Aunt Refilwe and she took me to the clinic. I can't believe I have gonorrhea! He said he was healthy."

*"If you had sex without a condom, you are always unprotected. You got gonorrhea from him."*

*"I know, I know. I hate him. He lied and made me sick. And I just wanted him to love me . . . I don't know anything about my real father except that he left you and that he is dead. Then my Daddy left and I thought he didn't love me either. I just wanted <u>someone</u> to love me."*

*"Your Daddy does love you. We had problems that we had to work out and now things are better between us. He has come home to stay because he loves us . . . all of us. He loves you so much, Kagiso."*

She hugged Kagiso and held her tight.

Kefentse continued, *"The STI that you got from that guy can be fully treated with medication and your Aunt Refilwe says you are not pregnant. But we need to return to the clinic in three months for an HIV test."*

*"HIV! I can't have HIV. He said he was healthy. No! I could die from that. I don't want to know if I have HIV!*

*"This is hard for both of us and it would be awful if you have the illness. But HIV can be managed now with ARV's and it is best if treatment is started early, so we need to know as soon as possible. More importantly, we have to take things one step at a time. We need to discuss this with your Daddy and together we will decide on the way forward.*

*"No, no. We can't tell him. I am scared for him to know. Don't tell him, please."*

*"I know that this is embarrassing for you, but Daddy and I are working as a team. Two heads are a lot better than one at times like these, and all three of us need to tackle this together. No one else needs to know what is going on."*

After sharing Kagiso's story with Tsiamo, the couple decided that the three of them would plan to go to the testing center together when the time was right. Kagiso needed parental consent to get an HIV test plus they wanted to provide support when the results came back, whatever here status.

Kagiso wanted to go right away and *"get the test over with."*

Her mother responded: *"I'll call the testing center and confirm the information I know about testing We need to wait three months before you can be accurately tested. You do know that HIV can be treated with ARV's now. right?*

*Kagiso nodded.*

*It was a very long three months before Kagiso, Kefentse and Tsiamo arrived at the clinic. The lady counselor at the testing center was friendly and helpful. Before the test, she gave them a lot of information to prepare them for the future, regardless of the outcome, and the blood was drawn. Even the short wait for the results were agonizing.*

*Kagiso murmured, "I would give anything or do anything to have this test be negative. I will never go through this again, because I will never again have unprotected sex."*

*The Counselor returned: "Good news. Your test is negative."*

*Kagiso sank into the chair with relief. She didn't hear much of the post-test counseling, and felt as if she were walking on air all the way home.*

*That evening after dinner, Tsiamo and Kefentse asked Kagiso to stay at the table and talk while Bopelo played with Ntume.*

*Kefentse began: "Of course, we all feel relieved that you are not sick, Kagiso, but there is something you must learn from this."*

*Tsiamo continued: "We all make mistakes. We are human. But if we don't grow from our mistakes, they are wasted. You know about my big mistake with that other woman. It shouldn't have happened, but it did, and afterwards, I felt terrible. I had to learn and grow from it. I think I have become a better person and a better parent."*

*"Daddy, I may not have been showing it, but I like the way you have been since you have been back from Ghanzi. I like it when you spend time with me."*

*"I like it too, Kagiso. It is something I am going to continue from now on. But what about you? You have been making some pretty scary mistakes lately. Have you learned anything?"*

*(Pause)*

*"Yes I have . . . I guess I have been screwing up and I know I have disappointed you both. I should have talked things over with you and from now on I know I will talk to you more about everything. I am sorry, Mama.*

*I am sorry, Daddy. I feel like I have been given a fresh start and I need to use it. I have learned that it is easy for someone to say they love you, but that there is a lot more to love than gifts, alcohol and sex. I also have been hanging out with the wrong kids at school. They said it was cool to dodge classes, be with an older guy and they drink a lot. I'm going to start being friends with Nonofo and Tumisang again. They were my best friends from CJSS but I dropped them. They are good girls. You are going to see a different Kagiso around here from now on."*

*Kefentse replied: "I hope that is true."*

*"It will be."*

*Kefentse went on: "You made a mistake, Kagiso but you were very fortunate."*

*Kefentse looked at Tsiamo.*

*Tsiamo spoke softly, "Kagiso, you were lucky . . .*

*I was not . . ."*

*Kagiso looked confused: "What do you mean?"*

*Tsiamo went on, "Your mother and I have talked. Because of what has happened, we think you are old enough to know about me. It is the right time . . . Kagiso, I have the virus. I am HIV positive."*

*"Oh no, Daddy . . . No!"*

*"Yes, it's true. That one mistake of sleeping with another woman cost me a lot. It cost me my health and nearly cost me my entire family. But your mother has taken me back even though I am HIV positive. I will have to take medication every day for the rest of my life and I have to live with the side effects. Your mother and I have to take precautions to make sure I don't pass HIV on to her. The doctor says if I take the medication faithfully and if I don't drink again, I can live a long life. Up until now, I haven't told anyone but your Mama. I didn't want to tell you or anybody else because I was embarrassed. I didn't know what people would think of me. I guess I also thought I was protecting you kids. I realize now that I was just protecting myself. Keeping this a secret has not been a help to you. AIDS is real and here in Botswana; now it is right here in our house. You are the first person other than your Mama who knows this. I will need to*

tell Bopelo and Ntume too, when they are older and when I think they can understand it."

Kagiso threw her arms around Tsiamo.

"Daddy I love you. You are the only Daddy I have ever known and I will always love you. I know from my HIV classes that there is no risk for any of us being in a house with a person who has HIV. And now I will need to remember everything else I learned so I can help you."

"Thank you, Kagiso. To fight this, I am going to need a lot of support. You are right. I am really at more risk of getting an illness from one of you, than you are of getting HIV from me. Since I found out, I have been learning about how to protect myself and live with this illness. HIV is not a death sentence any more, but it a heavy weight that I have to carry. It is something I will have to live with every day of my life."

They all sat quietly for a bit.

Kagiso turned to her parents, "Mama and Daddy, I wish I had heard these things earlier. Maybe if I had known that HIV is real and right here in our family, I wouldn't have gotten into trouble."

Kefentse responded: "I wish I had talked to you about a lot of things before now. I don't know if it would have changed the outcome for us, but looking back, I know it would have been better for you and more honest for me. Tsiamo, I am proud of you for disclosing your status. I wish more people could be as brave as you. This is the time for all of us to be open. No more secrets."

# CHAPTER 23

## GABORONE, BLOCK 7

*IN THE NEXT several months, Kefentse and Tsiamo noticed a marked difference in Kagiso. Her friends changed, her school grades and attendance improved and the whole family felt closer. In that time, Kagiso bravely asked about her real father. This was a question she had held for years, but had been afraid to ask. Now, with no secrets, she had the courage to ask her mother. Kefentse told Kagiso the whole story of Gape, her own early pregnancy with Kagiso and Gape's death, likely of AIDS.*

*Life did not stand still.*

*The family had to grow in many ways. Ntume was still too young, but within a few months, Tsiamo told Bopelo about his status. He also took a huge step by joining a support group for people living with AIDS. It was helpful for Tsiamo to know he was not alone.*

*Kagiso was true to her word and continued to get her life back on track. Her brush with possible HIV and having HIV in her immediate family energized her to become a more passionate and effective Peer Educator.*

*Kefentse and Tsiamo's marriage was stronger than ever and they were now taking a more active role in all aspects of their children's lives.*

As it is for all of us, being parents for Kefentse and Tsiamo had been challenging . . . but now they had the Power.

# Appendix 1

Resources on Male/Female Anatomy and Reproductive physiology:

Books:

Science is Fun . . . Standard 6, Moolman A. and Vermuelen J, Collegium
  Press

Science is Fun . . . Standard 7, Vermuelen J, Collegium Press

Science is Fun . . . Book 1, Moolman A. and Vermuelen J, Collegium
  Press

Internet Websites:

http://www.avert.org/puberty-sex.htm

http://web.jjay.cuny.edu/~acarpi/NSC/14-anatomy.htm

http://www.innerbody.com/image/repfov.html

http://www.innerbody.com/image/repmov.html

# APPENDIX 2

Selected research references supporting the concepts that the age of sexual debut increases and sexual activity in general decreases when age appropriate reproductive information is provided to children and parental intervention is active:

Commendador, Kathleen A. 2010 Parental Influences on Adolescent Decision Making and Contraceptive Use: Maternal Influence on Sexual Activity and Contraceptive Decision Making, Pediatr Nurs. ;36(3):147-156.

Kobak, R., Cole H, Fleming W, Ferenz-Gillies R. & Gamble W, 1993. Attachment and emotion regulation during mother-teen problem-solving: A control theory analysis. Child Development, 64, 231-245.

Koesten J, Miller KI, & Hummert ML, 2002 Family communication, self-efficacy and white adolescent females' risk behavior. Journal of Family Communication, Vol1, 7-27.

Miller, K, Fasula A., et al, 2009 Sexual Health Disparities among African American Youth and the Need for Early Prevention Approaches: Parenting and Youth Development Programs as Strategies for Pre-Risk. Prevention, The Journal of Equity in Health, November Vol. 2, No. 1, 19-28.

Miller K and Fasula A, et al, 2007 Barriers and Facilitators to Maternal Communication with Preadolescents about Age-Relevant Sexual Topics AIDS and Behavior, 365-374.

Pearson J, Muller C, and Frisco M, 2006. "Parental Involvement, Family Structure, and Adolescent Sexual Decision-Making." Sociological Perspectives, 49(1): 67-90.

Ramirez-Valles J, Zimmerman M, Juarez L, 2002 Gender Differences of Neighborhood and Social Control Processes: A Study of the Timing of First Intercourse Among Low Achieving, Urban, African-American Youth. Youth & Society, 33(3): 418-441.

Ramirez-Valles J, Zimmerman M, Newcomb M, 1998. Sexual Risk Behavior Among Youth: Modeling the Influence of Pro-social Activities and Socioeconomic Factors. Journal of Health and Social Behavior, 39: 237-253.

www.ingramcontent.com/pod-product-compliance
Lightning Source LLC
Chambersburg PA
CBHW020248290526
45784CB00003B/1157